CONTENTS

GAME BASICS	2
COMBAT TACTICS	6
CHARACTERS	8
EQUIPMENT	18
ENEMIES	29
WALKTHROUGH	40
STAGE 1: CENTRAL RAILROAD	42
STAGE 2: REMINESS GORGE	50
STAGE 3: HIESSGART	61
STAGE 4: NEW HIESSGART, PART 1	71
STAGE 5: NEW HIESSGART, PART 2	81
STAGE 6: NEW HIESSGART CASTLE	97
STAGE 7: HIESSGART ARMY FORTRESS	112
STAGE 8: UNDERGROUND WATERWAY	121
APPENDIX	142

FULLMETAL ALCHEMIST

—and the Broken Angel—

OFFICIAL STRATEGY GUIDE

BY RICK BARBA

Part 1: GETTING STARTED

Welcome to the official strategy guide for *Fullmetal Alchemist and the Broken Angel.* This first part of the book takes a look at the characters, weapons, enemies, items and accessories you'll encounter in the game. Part 2 takes you on a detailed, step by step walkthrough of each stage.

As we move forward, please keep in mind that this guide assumes you've read the excellent game manual and are familiar with the game's basic controls and functions. If you haven't done so yet, please do so now.

GAME BASICS

GAME BASICS
COMBAT TACTICS
CHARACTERS
EQUIPMENT
ENEMIES
WALKTHROUGH
APPENDIX

CONTROLS

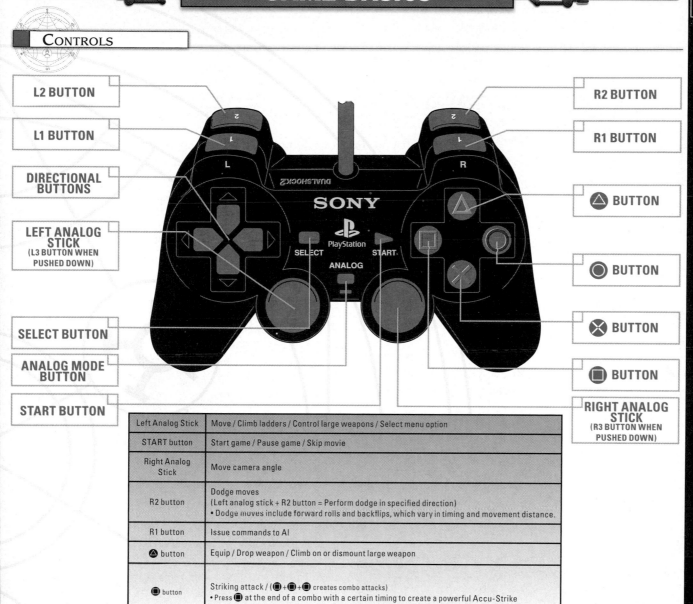

L2 BUTTON

L1 BUTTON

DIRECTIONAL BUTTONS

LEFT ANALOG STICK (L3 BUTTON WHEN PUSHED DOWN)

SELECT BUTTON

ANALOG MODE BUTTON

START BUTTON

R2 BUTTON

R1 BUTTON

△ BUTTON

● BUTTON

✕ BUTTON

■ BUTTON

RIGHT ANALOG STICK (R3 BUTTON WHEN PUSHED DOWN)

Left Analog Stick	Move / Climb ladders / Control large weapons / Select menu option
START button	Start game / Pause game / Skip movie
Right Analog Stick	Move camera angle
R2 button	Dodge moves (Left analog stick + R2 button = Perform dodge in specified direction) • Dodge moves include forward rolls and backflips, which vary in timing and movement distance.
R1 button	Issue commands to AI
△ button	Equip / Drop weapon / Climb on or dismount large weapon
■ button	Striking attack / (■+■+■ creates combo attacks) • Press ■ at the end of a combo with a certain timing to create a powerful Accu-Strike
● button	Transmute a Rockblocker (defensive) / Transmute a Stonespike (offensive) / Cancel

EXPLORATION

When you enter a new area, the first thing to do is clear out the baddies, of course. Step 2 is to check the post-combat health bar of both Ed and Al, and heal up if necessary. But before you move on, you should complete an important third step: *Search the area!*

Treasure chests have been scattered throughout each area. Look in every nook, cranny, and back alley. The extra Reloader (Metal) you find hidden under a pipe may turn out to be critically important in a boss battle later on.

SAVE POINTS

Glowing save points appear at multiple locations in each one of the game's eight stages. It is important to save your game *every time* you find a save point, even if it means replacing a previously saved game. The reason: Whenever you save your game, Ed and Al both restore their full HP. It's like finding a free Doubalixir (X) item every time.

STATUS

When you open the Menu screen and select Status, you can toggle between a series of numbers for each brother, Ed or Al. These numbers measure some important attributes that affect each brother's fighting and survival abilities.

	Name	Attribute	Description
THE STATS ARE:	VIT	Vitality	The higher this value, the greater your HP capacity. Your HP capacity equals the VIT value times 5.
	ATK	Attack	Affects the damage inflicted when the character uses hand-held weapons.
	DEF	Defense	Mitigates the damage done to the character by enemy strikes.
	ALC (Ed only)	Alchemy	Affects damage that Ed can inflict with his alchemy-based attacks.

GAINING EXPERIENCE (EXP) POINTS

Each time you defeat a foe, both Ed and Al gain experience in the form of EXP points from the victory. No matter *who* delivers more damage or *who* finally KO's the enemy, the amount of EXP gained from the victory is the same for both Ed and Al.

However, Ed can earn additional EXP by stringing together a linked series of hits called a *combo*. If you can execute a combo attack of more than 10 hits, Ed gains "Bonus EXP" points on top of the normal experience points earned from defeating the enemy.

The overall experience gained can change depending upon your method of defeating the enemy, too. For example, you can gain more EXP points by using a Cannon, Gatling Gun, or Crossbow versus whacking away with a handheld weapon.

For more on how combo attacks work, see "Combos" in the Combat Tactics section.

THE COMBO MAN

Only Ed can earn Bonus EXP points from executing combo attacks; AI cannot.

LEVELING UP

Once Ed or Al's EXP points pass a certain value (listed by NEXT on the Menu screen), that character's experience rating goes up one level. When you "level up," you boost each of the attributes listed on the Status screen (see the **Status** section above), and it becomes a bit easier to defeat opponents. Furthermore, you gain Bonus Points that you can distribute to Ed or Al.

BONUS POINTS

As mentioned, when you level up, you receive a certain number of Bonus Points. You can add these points to your Status attribute values—VIT, ATK, DEF, and (for Ed only) ALC—dividing them up between Ed's attributes and Al's attributes any way you wish. In other words, it's up to you how you choose to "raise" your characters.

BE SPENDTHRIFT WITH BONUS POINTS

You can even store Bonus Points without using them, if you want, although this strategy really has no benefit. *It is best to always allocate your bonus points as soon as you get them.*

Not only do you get Bonus Points when you level up, but you can also get them after a boss battle, depending on the Alchemist Rank you earn. Read on for more info on this aspect.

ALCHEMIST RANK

GAME BASICS

COMBAT TACTICS

CHARACTERS

EQUIPMENT

ENEMIES

WALKTHROUGH

APPENDIX

When you fight a boss, you earn one of four grades of Alchemist Rank depending upon your performance in that particular boss battle. The ranks, from highest to lowest, are: S, A, B, and C.

The computation of the rank changes from boss to boss, so your Alchemist Rank is higher if two things occur:

* Your time of battle is shorter

* Your Max Combo (number of hits in your longest combo string) is bigger

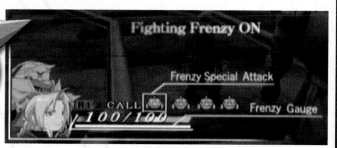

The number of Bonus Points you receive corresponds to the rank you receive. The higher the rank, the more bonus points received and likewise the lower the rank, the fewer bonus points received.

Alchemist Rank	Bonus Points Received:
S	3
A	2
B	1

COMBAT TACTICS

Before we get to the data tables and the game walkthrough, let's discuss a few aspects of combat in *Fullmetal Alchemist and the Broken Angel*. Fighting, after all, is the core of the game. So it helps to understand how the fighting works.

USING ALCHEMY

Rockblockers and Stonespikes

Ed's most basic alchemy skills allow him to create Rockblockers, which are temporary stone blocks used for defense or as jumping platforms. Just press the ● button once to create a Rockblocker.

Ed can also transmute an offensive weapon called a Stonespike. This is a formation of sharp rock spikes that shoot up from the ground in front of Ed, inflicting serious damage to enemies in the immediate vicinity. To create Stonespikes, hold down the ● button until the Alchemy Gauge is charged to red, then release.

The higher Ed's ALC rating, the more Rockblockers (up to three) he can transmute, and the more damage he can inflict with his Stonespike attack.

Using Transmuted Weapons

Weapons that Ed creates via alchemy from other objects found on the map are called "transmuted weapons." Transmuted weapons come in a wide variety of forms. Some have very fast combo attacks (like the Dagger) while others perform deadly single strikes (like the Katana).

Elemental Effects

Some handheld weapons in the game can be enhanced by the elemental effects of Wind, Lightning, or Fire. Fire damage causes DOT (Damage Over Time). Lightning damage can cause enemies to become paralyzed. Wind speeds up the weapon's attack letting you get in multiple hits. All elemental enhanced weapons will do more damage to obvious weaker enemies. Many stronger, higher-level enemies have resistances to elemental attacks.

Special Attacks (Ed & Al)

The game manual describes how to trigger a Special Attack with Ed and Al. These attacks are particularly effective when the boys are surrounded by numerous enemies. The problem is, to trigger a Special Attack you need Ed's Alchemy Gauge charged up to red. If an enemy strikes Ed, the gauge resets back to zero, so you have to charge it again from scratch. Obviously, this could happen again and again if Ed is surrounded by aggressive enemies, making it very hard to trigger the Special Attack!

One way to trigger this is to keep Ed *moving, rolling, dodging* and pressing the R2 button repeatedly) while *at the same time* you hold down the ● button to charge up the Alchemy Gauge. Once the gauge is red and ready, run near Al or call him over to you (whichever location has the most enemies to whack) and then press the R1 button to trigger the Special Attack.

Reviving Al

If Al runs out of HP, he falls to the ground, knocked out. Al revives on his own after a minute or so, but Ed can revive him immediately using alchemy. Just approach Al and hold down the ● button. When Ed is inside Al's energy ring, release the button to revive Al. He says, "I thought I was dead!" and then fights on with his HP fully restored.

DODGING & BREAKFALLING

Two of the most critical fighting skills you can master have absolutely nothing to do with hitting the other guy. First, you cannot lose a fight if you never get hit, so learning to perfect the artful dodge is a worthwhile endeavor. Just press the R2 button while moving the analog stick in the direction you wish to roll. Dodging lets you avoid most blows, including even wide area attacks that would otherwise knock you senseless.

Second, if you do take a shot, it's nice if you can avoid the dangerous downtime that comes from getting knocked off your feet. Simple enough—just press the ✖ button right before Ed hits the ground. If you time it well, Ed pops right back up and shouts, "No problem!" Such resilience is a thing of beauty, isn't it?

As we mentioned earlier, Ed can earn additional EXP by stringing together a linked series of strikes called a *combo*. If Ed can string together combo attacks with more than 10 hits on targeted foes, he gains "Bonus EXP" points on top of the normal experience points earned from defeating the enemy.

Note that combos do not *strengthen* attacks, but rather net Ed some Bonus EXP points. Each hit of a combo attack does the same damage as a normal individual attack. However, combos are extremely effective attack techniques, because the very short time between hits allows the targeted enemy little opportunity for a counterstrike.

This is especially true in the case of a combo with alchemy attacks sandwiched in-between weapon strikes. While administering such a combo string attack, you are virtually invulnerable.

Combo Strings

If you want to earn some serious Bonus EXP points, a single combo will be insufficient. You need to string together a series of combos in order to rack up enough hits for some big, bonus EXP rewards.

To increase the number of hits in a combo:

ONE: Don't end the combo until the enemy is KO'd.

The last hit in a combo usually knocks your enemy down or out of range. In other words, once you perform your last strike, the next few swings won't connect (because the enemy is down) and thus your combo string will end. So you have to learn how to *not strike your final blow* in order to increase the number of consecutive hits and extend a combo string.

For example, the Lance and the Sword each perform a basic 3-hit combo attack if you press the ● button quickly three times. Make sure to stop your attack after the second hit, wait a brief moment (not *too* long), get in two more strikes, pause again, strike twice more, and so on.

TWO: Become skillful at hitting multiple targets with fast-firing weapons.

The truth is that it's far easier to increase the number of hits in a combo when you are using the Gatling Gun or Crossbow rather than with a handheld weapon. Once you've put a target in your sights, just keep firing, holding down ● as the projectiles fly on their way to the target. In this way, it's really easy to build up hits. The Gatling Gun, for example, can fire up to 80 bullets. If you can hit a target or targets with all 80 bullets and little time between hits, you can earn a nice, big Bonus EXP reward.

An Accu-Strike results from a perfectly timed strike at the end of a combo attack. When you perform a sequence of attacks in a combo string, then press the ● button to coincide with the last strike of your combo, Ed executes the Accu-Strike. The attack power of an Accu-Strike is 1.5 times stronger than a normal strike.

The secret is to carefully watch the last attack and press ● just at the moment Ed raises the weapon over his head for the final stroke. The weapon begins to glow and you see a flash when the Accu-Strike occurs. There is an item you get in the game called the Armlet of Accuracy that, when equipped, automatically performs Accu-Strikes for you.

GAME BASICS

COMBAT TACTICS

CHARACTERS

EQUIPMENT

ENEMIES

WALKTHROUGH

APPENDIX

FIGHTING FRENZY

When Ed and Al attack opponents, their blue Frenzy Gauge begins to build up. When the gauge is full, it flashes rainbow colors indicating that a "Fighting Frenzy" has been triggered. During that time all sorts of special things happen, such as a nice increase in ATK (attack) power and increase in EXP (experience) points acquired from defeating foes.

Perhaps the biggest benefit of a Fighting Frenzy state is the ability to trigger a Frenzy Special Attack, a powered up version of the Special Attack. When Ed and Al execute one of these spectacular attacks, all monsters in the immediate area might as well kiss their tails goodbye.

Always do your best to make a Fighting Frenzy state last as long as possible to keep the advantage it provides. The state continues until one of the following conditions is met:

* Ed gets knocked to the ground (unless you negate the fall with a successful "Breakfall" move)

* Either Ed or Al reaches 0 HP

* A Frenzy Special Attack is used

* Full HP restored at a save point

* The stage is cleared

CHARACTERS

Edward Elric

Alphonse Elric

Armony Eiselstein

Professor Wilhelm Eiselstein

Alex Luis Armstrong

Roy Mustang

Riza Hawkeye

Senior Colonel Genz Bresslau

Brigadier Mudi Nemda

Camilla

Time to meet the main characters of *Fullmetal Alchemist and the Broken Angel*. For each character, we start off with the official bio from the game manual, then add a few comments of our own.

Ed is a quick-tempered fellow, prone to outbursts of what a charitable person might term "enthusiasm." When the going gets tough, Ed is a true star, even if his first instinct is to start swinging and ask questions later. His alchemy powers are prodigious, and should be used freely.

EDWARD
ELRIC

A fifteen-year-old prodigy who became

the youngest State Alchemist in history. His alias, "Fullmetal," derives from the fact

that his right arm and left leg are metallic, artificial limbs known as automail. He

and his younger brother Alphonse are on a journey to find the Philosopher's Stone,

which may hold the power for them to regain their bodies.

GAME BASICS

COMBAT TACTICS

CHARACTERS

EQUIPMENT

ENEMIES

WALKTHROUGH

APPENDIX

ALPHONSE ELRIC

Sure, Al may have a "gentle heart," but he is no slouch on the field of battle. His tackle-attack is formidable, and his aim when he's assigned to a Cannon or Crossbow is perfect, for the most part. Keep transmuting weapons for Al and he can be your mighty fighting companion.

Inside the giant suit of armor is a soul of a fourteen-year-old boy with a gentle heart. He journeys with his older brother Edward in hope that the both of them will regain their original bodies. Always calm and stable in character, Al is the one who chides Ed, who is quick to lose his cool. Al is Ed's perfect companion.

CHARACTERS

Edward Elric

Alphonse Elric

Armony Eiselstein

Professor Wilhelm Eiselstein

Alex Luis Armstrong

Roy Mustang

Riza Hawkeye

Senior Colonel Genz Bresslau

Brigadier Mudi Nemda

Camilla

Armony's relationship to Ed is the engine that drives the story forward in this game. His first impression of her is not too good, but her desire to learn alchemy and the poignant circumstances of her life lead Ed to a somewhat different, if bittersweet, conclusion.

ARMONY EISELSTEIN

Wilhelm Eiselstein's daughter.

Wilhelm has forbidden her from learning alchemy on the basis that she has no talent. She believes her father is harsh toward her because she is inept at the ancient science. To gain recognition from her father, she becomes an apprentice to Edward.

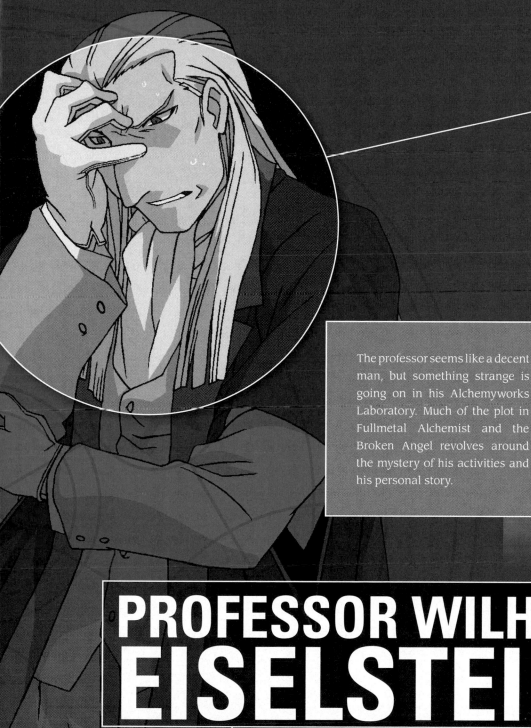

GAME BASICS

COMBAT TACTICS

CHARACTERS

EQUIPMENT

ENEMIES

WALKTHROUGH

APPENDIX

The professor seems like a decent man, but something strange is going on in his Alchemyworks Laboratory. Much of the plot in Fullmetal Alchemist and the Broken Angel revolves around the mystery of his activities and his personal story.

PROFESSOR WILHELM
EISELSTEIN

One of the Ten Alchemists, and a renowned authority on catalytics, the study of making alchemy more efficient. He is now conducting research on the Philosopher's Catalyst, a legendary material comparable in power to the Philosopher's Stone. When the town of Hiessgart came under the attack of chimeras, he brought the refugees to safety and led the efforts in building New Hiessgart.

CHARACTERS

Edward Elric

Alphonse Elric

Armony Eiselstein

Professor Wilhelm Eiselstein

Alex Luis Armstrong

Roy Mustang

Riza Hawkeye

Senior Colonel Genz Bresslau

Brigadier Mudi Nemda

Camilla

Major Armstrong has been assigned to oversee the travels and activities of the Elric boys, and his relationship to them is like an uncle. Quiet and restrained normally, he becomes an animated, dynamic (and suddenly shirtless) force when push comes to shove. His alchemy powers are fierce and commanding.

ALEX LUIS
ARMSTRONG

A major in the military. He is capable

of fancy footwork despite his burly physique. His giant knuckles enable him

to perform powerful alchemy, for which this State Alchemist has been given

the alias "The Strong-Armed Alchemist."

GAME BASICS

COMBAT TACTICS

CHARACTERS

EQUIPMENT

ENEMIES

WALKTHROUGH

APPENDIX

ROY MUSTANG

A military colonel and State Alchemist who goes by the nickname "The Flame Alchemist." His gloves are made of pyrotex, which he uses to create alchemy-controlled flames.

Mustang commands a lot of respect in the State Alchemy office, and the Elric boys are his direct charge. He's not above using them for his indirect purposes, however.

CHARACTERS

Edward Elric

Alphonse Elric

Armony Eiselstein

Professor Wilhelm Eiselstein

Alex Luis Armstrong

Roy Mustang

Riza Hawkeye

Senior Colonel Genz Bresslau

Brigadier Mudi Nemda

Camilla

Lieutenant Hawkeye plays a prominent undercover role in unraveling the mystery of New Hiessgart Castle. Note: Once you beat the game, be sure to view her highly detailed report after the post-game credits run.

RIZA HAWKEYE

A military lieutenant,

and a close aide to the Colonel. A woman

highly capable in any assignment, Hawkeye

is secretly feared by her peers for her

imperturbable manner.

GAME BASICS

COMBAT TACTICS

CHARACTERS

EQUIPMENT

ENEMIES

WALKTHROUGH

APPENDIX

Genz is one of the bosses you fight in the game. As a matter of fact, you fight Genz *three* different times in the game. His reincarnations are increasingly deadly and "metallic" in nature.

SENIOR COLONEL GENZ
BRESSLAU

A military policeman who proclaims

himself to be "The Armor-Piercing Alchemist" and the strongest in

the military. He has no interest in rank or honor; his only pursuit is

his own physical strength. He is quick to anger, and shows no mercy

for subordinates who fail in their duty.

CHARACTERS

Edward Elric
Alphonse Elric
Armony Eiselstein
Professor Wilhelm Eiselstein
Alex Luis Armstrong
Roy Mustang
Riza Hawkeye
Senior Colonel Genz Bresslau
Brigadier Mudi Nemda
Camilla

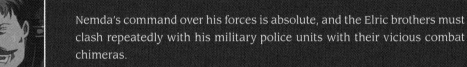

Nemda's command over his forces is absolute, and the Elric brothers must clash repeatedly with his military police units with their vicious combat chimeras.

BRIGADIER MUDI
NEMDA

Chief of the military police

in the Hiessgart region. Tenacious in expanding his own power, he has almost completely privatized the army. His ambition is to build his own Nemda Kingdom.

GAME BASICS

COMBAT TACTICS

CHARACTERS

EQUIPMENT

ENEMIES

WALKTHROUGH

APPENDIX

CAMILLA

A mysterious woman dressed

in black. Old records describe her as a legendary alchemist

who disappeared several decades ago...

Enough said!

WEAPONS

Fullmetal Alchemist features quite an arsenal of weaponry that can be transmuted from everyday objects—64 in all. When you hold down the ◉ button, icons appear above each nearby transmutable object indicating weapons it can become. Learn to distinguish between icons, and get in the habit of holding down the ◉ button as you run around an area so you can see what is available.

For each weapon listed below, the damage inflicted by a single hit is represented on a scale of 1 to 5 symbols. Note that the attack power of items that excel in quick, rapid hits is still calculated by the strength of each individual hit.

ED'S HANDHELD WEAPONS

LANCE

This is the first transmuted weapon Ed gets his hands on in the game. The standard Lance has a good reach, so Ed can score direct hits from just out of enemy counterattack range. Another nice benefit of your Lance attack is the ability to hit targets a step below your position, thus you get one additional whack at fallen enemies.

LIGHTNING LANCE

When you imbue your standard Lance with the added power of a Lightning Element, a jolting hit can temporarily paralyze a target, freezing the enemy in his tracks for a few seconds.

DAGGER

Although its attack power and range are small, the trusty Dagger is very well suited for fast attacks. It is the best weapon for combo attacks—that is, for scoring strings of hits with no time between to earn combo EXP bonuses. (The Plastic Hammer gives you easier combos, but inflicts very little damage.)

WIND DAGGER

The ultimate combo weapon! This is your standard Dagger with the added speed of an imbued Wind Element. Indeed, the Wind Dagger's attack speed is insanely fast, and thus your ability to create long combo strings increases accordingly.

SWORD

This big blade features a high attack power *and* a wide attack swath. When used in a combo, the Sword mows down all surrounding enemies.

FIRE SWORD

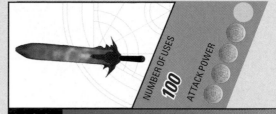

Your basic Sword with the added power of the Fire Element. Fire increases the weapon's attack power and is particularly effective against water-based enemies.

PLASTIC HAMMER

No matter how high your ATK attribute is, this weapon can only deliver 1 point of damage per hit. Although it has practically no attack power, the Plastic Hammer is absolutely unrivalled in its attack speed and therefore offers an excellent way to earn combo bonuses. Against a slow, heavy foe like a Tank, you can link dozens of hits in a single combo string.

BOOMERANG

When thrown at enemies, the Boomerang hits with surprising power, then returns automatically to Ed's hand. Out of all handheld weapons, this one has the farthest ranged attack. When you catch the returning boomerang, you are defenseless for a moment, so it's best to attack more distant enemies. Aiming can be tricky, too. Ed throws the Boomerang *directly* forward from his current orientation, so you must turn him to face his intended target.

WIND BOOMERANG

Same as the Boomerang with the added speed of the Wind Element. Like the regular Boomerang, it can hit a target going out when first tossed, and then hit again as it returns to Ed's hand. Since a single attack can do multiple hits, it is well suited for combos.

BOW & ARROW

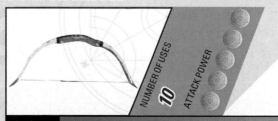

The Bow & Arrow is a nice middle-ranged distance weapon for Ed. To use it, hold down the ● button to switch to a first-person "crosshairs" view, then release the button to fire. The Bow has extremely high attack power, but its unique viewpoint can be problematic in a fierce melee situation. You can see only in front of you, so resourceful enemies might slip around you and attack from behind. When using this weapon, it's best to have something solid like a wall behind your back.

GAME BASICS
COMBAT TACTICS
CHARACTERS
EQUIPMENT
WEAPONS
ITEMS
ACCESSORIES
WALKTHROUGH
APPENDIX

SHOCKWAVE HOPPER

NUMBER OF USES **UNLIMITED** ATTACK POWER

Fun but deadly, the Shockwave Hopper inflicts area damage on all enemies in your vicinity. Press the ● button just as you hit the ground to accelerate your next bounce upward. If you get high enough, the Hopper hits the ground the next time with a shock wave. You can jump three different levels into the air. The higher you jump, the wider the attack range and the higher the attack power.

Tip: The Shockwave Hopper is actually somewhat maneuverable while airborne. On your highest jump, your hang-time is fairly long, so push the left analog stick in the direction of those enemies!

RAZOR RING

NUMBER OF USES **UNLIMITED** ATTACK POWER

Like the Boomerang, the Razor Ring is a throwing weapon that automatically returns to you. Although not quite as far-ranged as the Boomerang, this weapon can still travel quite a distance. And it's really three weapons in one. You get three rings when you equip the Razor Ring, and you can throw all three in a row. This is great way to keep multiple enemies on the defensive.

WIND RAZOR RING

NUMBER OF USES **50** ATTACK POWER

This is your standard Razor Ring with the added speed of the Wind Element. Since a single attack can inflict a number of hits, it is well suited for combos.

DEADLY BUBBLES

NUMBER OF USES **10** ATTACK POWER

For a brief time, you can seal an enemy inside a bubble with this "weapon." It won't hurt enemies, but you can use it to avoid unnecessary battles when you are low on HP. This defensive bubble won't let enemy attacks through. Thus you can rest just a little bit during a grueling battle.

AL'S HANDHELD WEAPONS

GAME BASICS

COMBAT TACTICS

CHARACTERS

EQUIPMENT

WEAPONS

ITEMS

ACCESSORIES

WALKTHROUGH

APPENDIX

LANCE

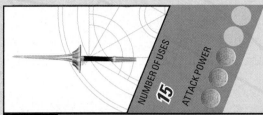

NUMBER OF USES **15** · ATTACK POWER

One of Al's exclusive basic weapons. Just like Ed's own Lance, it can attack from a good distance. Since it can only attack in a straight line, however, it puts Al at a disadvantage when he's surrounded by enemies.

FIRE LANCE

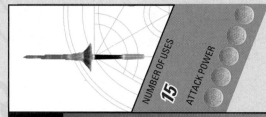

NUMBER OF USES **15** · ATTACK POWER

The basic Lance with the added power of the Fire Element. Attack power is increased significantly and it can add additional fire damage over time.

LIGHTNING LANCE

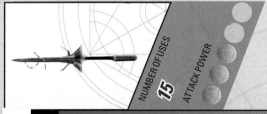

NUMBER OF USES **15** · ATTACK POWER

Al's Lance is imbued with the added power of the Lightning Element. Attack power is increased and it can cause paralysis, temporarily stopping an enemy's movements.

SWORD

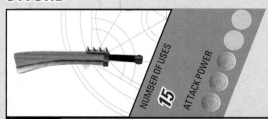

NUMBER OF USES **15** · ATTACK POWER

One of Al's exclusive basic weapons. Although shaped somewhat like a long hatchet, it has the widest range of attack and is highly versatile.

FIRE SWORD

NUMBER OF USES **15** · ATTACK POWER

Standard Sword with the added power of the Fire Element. Attack power is increased and it can add additional fire damage over time.

LIGHTNING SWORD

NUMBER OF USES **15** · ATTACK POWER

Standard Sword with the added power of the Lightning Element. Attack power is increased and it can cause paralysis, temporarily stopping an enemy's movements.

PICKAXE

NUMBER OF USES **15** ATTACK POWER

Leaves many gaps in an attack, but has very high attack power. Even if the main attack misses, an enemy may be damaged by debris flying up from the pickaxe ground strike.

HAMMER

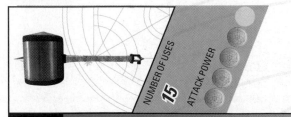

NUMBER OF USES **15** ATTACK POWER

Since it has the potential of hitting more than one enemy, this weapon is highly useful when enemies are massed together. The giant Hammer has the highest attack power of any of Al's exclusive weapons.

ED OR AL
HANDHELD WEAPONS

KATANA

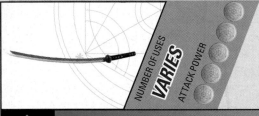

NUMBER OF USES **VARIES** ATTACK POWER

This weapon has the ability to cause instant death to an enemy, but if it scores a one-hit kill it may automatically disappear. So it must be used with great care. You should have another weapon ready on the side.

TORCH

NUMBER OF USES **10** ATTACK POWER

If you throw a torch at an enemy, you set him on fire for a short time and he receives damage. Oil also drips out of the torch and this oil can be set on fire.

GRENADE

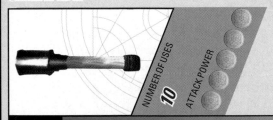

NUMBER OF USES **10** ATTACK POWER

Just like the Torch, but far more powerful, the Grenade is ideal for dealing area damage to entire packs of enemies. A Grenade explodes in about three seconds, or if it touches an enemy. Watch your enemy's movement and time the attack well!

FLAMETHROWER

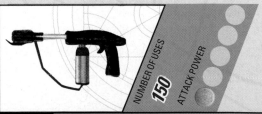

NUMBER OF USES **150** ATTACK POWER

A single shot is insignificant, but this weapon's strong point is the ease with which you can perform combos. If you use it continuously it'll run out of fuel quickly, so keep an eye on your ammunition number!

LARGE (TURRETS & VEHICLES)

GAME BASICS
COMBAT TACTICS
CHARACTERS
EQUIPMENT
WEAPONS
ITEMS
ACCESSORIES
WALKTHROUGH
APPENDIX

Note that either brother can mount and use these weapons, but the attack power goes down if Al is aboard. Ed's potency with large transmuted weapons goes up as his ALC stat rises.

CROSSBOW

NUMBER OF USES: 30 — ATTACK POWER: Lv.1 / Lv.2

The Crossbow is a large transmutation that you can swivel and fire simultaneously. You can replenish its ammunition by expending a Reloader (Wood). The Lv. 2 version increases the attack power slightly.

QUINTUPLE CROSSBOW

NUMBER OF USES: 80 — ATTACK POWER

Firing this Crossbow releases five arrows per shot. Each individual hit is relatively weak, but hitting a target with all five arrows of one shot can do considerable damage. Replenish ammunition with a Reloader (Wood) just like the standard Crossbow.

CANNON

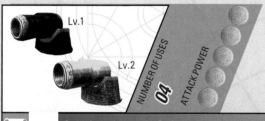

NUMBER OF USES: 04 — ATTACK POWER

Another type of large transmutation, the Cannon can fire only four shots. However, its shells hit with great power, and you can replenish its ammunition with a Reloader (Metal).

GATLING GUN

NUMBER OF USES: 80 — ATTACK POWER

Gatling Gun shots are weak individually. But this rapid-firing weapon pumps out an awesome 80 shots before requiring a reload. Use this weapon against bosses to rack up big combos and help obtain an Alchemist Rank of "S."

STEAMROLLER

NUMBER OF USES: UNLIMITED — ATTACK POWER

The front roller section deals good damage to enemies and flattens them momentarily. Compared to a tank it can make some tight turns, so on flat surfaces it's also quite convenient for getting around.

TANK

NUMBER OF USES: 10 — ATTACK POWER

The Tank features a powerful cannon fired using the attack button. This vehicle cannot make tight turns, but is useful when you need to deal a lot of heavy damage. Careful though! The Tank's cannon can also deal damage to Ed and Al. Be sure the target isn't too close when you fire!

AUTONOMOUS

POISON COW

NUMBER OF USES **01**

ATTACK POWER

For a short time, this mechanical unit moves on its own, letting loose a poison bubble attack. Ed and Al can take damage from it too, so be sure to avoid the pink bubbles! Once it stops moving, you can transmute it into an Elixir (S) item.

MINE/LARGE MINE

NUMBER OF USES **01**

ATTACK POWER

Lv.2

A portable land mine that you can pick up and carry by hand, it flares up and explodes once an enemy comes within range. You can also cause it to explode by attacking it.

TRIPLE MINES/LARGE TRIPLE MINES

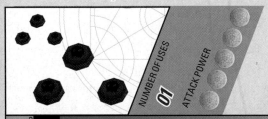

NUMBER OF USES **01**

ATTACK POWER

x3

x3
Lv.2

Created by transmuting a land mine or a large land mine, the attack power remains the same, but with 3 times as many units, you can damage more enemies.

LIGHTNING MINE/
LARGE LIGHTNING MINE

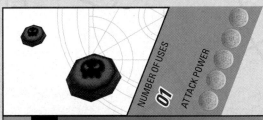

NUMBER OF USES **01**

ATTACK POWER

Lv.2

This is a mine imbued with the Lightning Element. When enemies trigger it, it explodes and immobilizes them for a short time.

TRIPLE LIGHTNING MINE/
LARGE TRIPLE LIGHTNING MINE

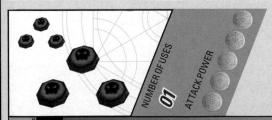

NUMBER OF USES **01**

ATTACK POWER

x3

x3
Lv.2

Created by transmuting a Lightning Mine, or Large Lightning Mine. If you note your foe's movement patterns and place it well, this trio of mines can cause tremendous damage.

STEEL BALL

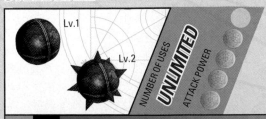

Lv.1

Lv.2

NUMBER OF USES **UNLIMITED**

ATTACK POWER

The Steel Ball rolls forward to attack enemies, dealing loads of damage to enemies in its path. Keep in mind that Ed and Al are also susceptible to damage, so be careful where you use it!

STEEL BALL (FIRE)

This Steel Ball has been imbued with a Flame Element. It's used in the same way as the standard Steel Ball but, since it's engulfed in flames, anyone who touches it will be set ablaze.

SUCTION MACHINE

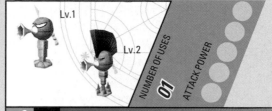

After transmuting this device, press the ⚠ button to activate it. For a few seconds it sucks in enemies and gathers them into a tight group. If you transmute it again after it stops sucking, it becomes an Elixir (S) item.

SUCTION MACHINE (FIRE)

A Suction Machine imbued with a Flame Element. After it stops sucking in enemies, it creates a quick blaze that damages them.

SUCTION MACHINE (WIND)

A Suction Machine imbued with a Wind Element. After it stops sucking in enemies, it creates a whirlwind that damages them.

BOMB

This time bomb will ignite when hit and explodes around 10 seconds later. When it flashes red, it's going to blow soon so push it towards the enemy!

DUMMY ED

This device creates a duplicate Ed that walks around to distract the enemy. If enemies hit it a certain number of times it loses its form, but you can also transmute it into an Elixir (S) item afterwards.

DUMMY ED (POISON)

This version of the Dummy Ed afflicts its attackers with poison. There are very few of these in the game, making it a rare and valuable transmutation.

DUMMY ED (FIRE)

This version of the Dummy Ed inflicts flame damage to its attackers. Compared to the poison version, this one is more commonplace and can be found and transmuted in many areas.

GAME BASICS

COMBAT TACTICS

CHARACTERS

EQUIPMENT

WEAPONS

ITEMS

ACCESSORIES

WALKTHROUGH

APPENDIX

WASHTUB

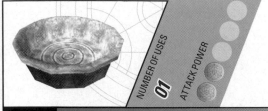

When you transmute a Washtub, it is automatically used to attack an enemy. You can't count on its attack power, but it will automatically track and hit the enemy. The attack area of this rarely seen object is small, so try to pack in enemies tightly!

FIRE HYDRANT

After transmuting this item, approach it and press the ● button to operate it. For a short time it rotates and sprays water in a circular area to deal damage. It will also hurt Ed and Al, so be sure to move away once it goes off!

MONOLITH/TOTEMPOLE BLOCKS

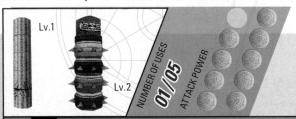

After you transmute a Monolith, attack it in the direction you want it to fall and it will topple over. In the Totempole's case, you deal damage to an enemy by whacking and launching one section at a time.

STEEL TRAP

Enemies that step into the Steel Trap remain unable to move for a short time. It's best suited for stopping fast enemies in their tracks, letting you unload on them with quick combo attacks until the trap wears off.

STICKY OIL

After you transmute the Sticky Oil canister, attack it to spill oil over the area. Enemies that step onto the oil remain stuck for several seconds. (This holds true for Ed and Al too, so be careful.) Furthermore, you can set it on fire with a Torch, Grenade, Flamethrower or other flaming object.

ITEMS

Fullmetal Alchemist features various types of items, from elixirs that heal your HP, to herbs that negate or cure various status ailments, to special elements that imbue your weapons with extra potency. Items are either dropped by defeated enemies or found in treasure chests. When you pick them up, items automatically go into your Item inventory. During the game, you can hit Pause and select "Item" on the Menu Screen to view and use your items.

CHEST HUNT
Many useful items, some rare, are stashed in treasure chests scattered throughout each area. Search for chests carefully!

GAME BASICS

COMBAT TACTICS

CHARACTERS

EQUIPMENT

WEAPONS

ITEMS

ACCESSORIES

WALKTHROUGH

APPENDIX

ITEM DATA

Item	Category	Effect
Elixir (S)	Single Recovery	Restores 100 HP to Ed or Al.
Elixir (M)	Single Recovery	Restores 200 HP to Ed or Al.
Elixir (L)	Single Recovery	Restores 400 HP to Ed or Al.
Elixir (X)	Single Recovery	Fully restores all HP to Ed or Al.
Doubalixir (S)	Pair Recovery	Restores 100 HP to both characters.
Doubalixir (M)	Pair Recovery	Restores 200 HP to both characters.
Doubalixir (L)	Pair Recovery	Restores 400 HP to both characters.
Doubalixir (X)	Pair Recovery	Fully restores all HP to both characters.
Relax-Herb	Status Ailment	Negates paralysis.
Detox-Herb	Status Ailment	Cures poison.
Equip-Herb	Status Ailment	Allows user to equip transmuted weapons.
ALC-Herb	Status Ailment	Allows Ed to transmute items.
ATK-Caps	Ability Enhancer	Increases ATK. Effects limited to current area. Max use: 1 per area.
ALC-Caps	Ability Enhancer	Increases ALC. Effects limited to current area. Max use: 1 per area.
DEF-Caps	Ability Enhancer	Increases DEF. Effects limited to current area. Max use: 1 per area.
AGL-Caps	Ability Enhancer	Increases AGL. Effects limited to current area. Max use: 1 per area.
Magic-Caps	Ability Enhancer	Increases ATK, ALC, DEF, AGL. Effects limited to current area. Max use: 1 per area.
Frenzy Potion	Ability Enhancer	Activates Fighting Frenzy.
Special Potion	Ability Enhancer	Adds one special attack icon to your HP bar.
Growth Seed	Ability Enhancer	Grants additional Bonus Points when the player levels up.
Reloader (Wood)	Reload	Allows Ed to reload a previously used Crossbow by re-transmuting it.
Reloader (Metal)	Reload	Allows Ed to reload a previously used Cannon, Gatling Gun, or Tank by re-transmuting it.
Fire Element	Additional Effects	Allows Ed to add Fire properties to weapons through alchemy.
Wind Element	Additional Effects	Allows Ed to add Wind properties to weapons through alchemy.
Lightning Element	Additional Effects	Allows Ed to add Lightning properties to weapons through alchemy.

ACCESSORIES

Unlike Items, Accessories are objects that you can equip and that, once found, do not disappear, not even when used. Most of the accessories in *Fullmetal Alchemist and the Broken Angel* either boost a particular attribute or bestow some special effect. Obtain them from treasure chests or by beating a boss. Ed and Al can equip two accessories apiece.

ACCESSORIZING FOR THE BOSS

Before a boss battle, always double-check the accessories you have equipped. Then, if necessary, re-equip to cover your weak spots.

ACCESSORIES DATA

Accessory	Used By	Description
Lead Ring	Both	Increases VIT by 5.
Silver Ring	Both	Increases VIT by 10.
Gold Ring	Both	Increases VIT by 15.
Fullmetal Ring	Both	Increases VIT by 20.
Double-Edged Ring	Both	Doubles max HP, but decreases other attributes by 50 percent.
Lead Bangle	Both	Increase ATK by 1.
Silver Bangle	Both	Increase ATK by 3.
Gold Bangle	Both	Increase ATK by 5.
Fullmetal Bangle	Both	Increase ATK by 7.
Double-Edged Bangle	Both	Increases ATK by 25 percent, but decreases DEF and ALC by 50 percent.
Lead Plate	Both	Increases DEF by 1.
Silver Plate	Both	Increases DEF by 3.
Gold Plate	Both	Increases DEF by 5.
Fullmetal Plate	Both	Increases DEF by 7.
Double-Edged Armor	Both	Increases DEF by 25 percent, but decreases ATK and ALC by 50 percent.
Steel Armor	Both	Reduces all damage types by 5 percent.
Alchemy Armor	Both	Reduces alchemic damage by 25%.
Bulletproof Vest	Both	Reduces gun damage by 25 percent.
Lead Earrings	Ed	Increases ALC by 1.
Silver Earrings	Ed	Increases ALC by 3.
Gold Earrings	Ed	Increases ALC by 5.
Fullmetal Earrings	Ed	Increases ALC by 7.
Double-Edged Earrings	Ed	Increases ALC by 25 percent, but decreases ATK and DEF by 50 percent.
Armlet of Accuracy	Both	Automates Accu-Strikes.
Armlet of Strength	Both	Knocks most enemies into the air to facilitate juggle attacks.
Armlet of Prowess	Both	Knocks most enemies down when an attack connects.
Armlet of Penetration	Both	Allows you to strike blocking enemies. Decreases ATK by 10 percent.
Armlet of Absorption	Both	Increases your HP bar by 5 percent of the damage points you deal.
Armlet of Consecution	Both	Facilitates combo attacks.
Armlet of Debilitation	Both	Always deals 1 HP of damage when you attack.

ACCESSORIES DATA (CON'T)

Accessory	Used By	Description
Alchemic Crystal	Ed	Increases Alchemy Gauge regeneration speed.
Amulet	Ed	Revives Ed when he is KO'd. Breaks after one use.
Moon Medal	Both	Increases all attributes by 10 percent.
Sun Medal	Both	Increases all attributes by 20%.
Grindstone	Al	Allows unlimited use of equipped weapons (except Katana).
Tall Boots	Ed	Increases EXP and boosts all attributes by 3%.
Glass Samurai	Ed	All attributes drop 90%, but allows for unlimited Katana attacks.
Demon Fist	Al	All attributes drop 50%, but barehanded attacks can instantly kill an enemy.
Bond of Brotherhood	Both	Increases the ATK of special attacks.
Cologne	Both	Attracts enemies with its irresistible scent.
Cloak	Both	Prevents enemies from easily detecting the wearer.
Lucky Bag	Both	Increases the chances of defeated enemies dropping items.
Red Loincloth	Al	Increases ATK by 25%, but prevents Al from responding to Ed's orders.
White Loincloth	Al	Prevents Al from attacking on his own, but still allows for following and tackling.
Ripped Loincloth	Al	Allows Al to dodge most enemies.
Training Manual	Both	Increases EXP gained by 5 percent.
Brawling Guide	Ed	Increases ATK by 15 percent, but blocks the accumulation of combo bonus EXP.
Alchemy Guide	Ed	Increases normal EXP gained by 50 percent if you defeat enemy via alchemy.
Combo Guide	Ed	Increases normal EXP gained and combo bonus EXP gained with +10-hit combos.
Ultra Combo Guide	Ed	Increases normal EXP gained and combo bonus EXP gained with +20-hit combos.
Flurry Guide	Ed	Triples combo bonus EXP, but cuts normal EXP gained in half.

Here's a good look at the enemies, both human and chimera, that confront Edward and Alphonse Elric along the course of *Fullmetal Alchemist and the Broken Angel*. The foes here are presented according to their introduction in the story, but keep in mind that enemy types who appear in earlier stages sometimes reappear later.

GAME BASICS

COMBAT TACTICS

CHARACTERS

EQUIPMENT

ENEMIES

WALKTHROUGH

APPENDIX

STAGE 1

TRAIN HIJACKER (SWORD)

A member of the People's Eastern Revolution Front that has taken over the Central-bound train, this thug wears a blue handana and wields a menacing sword from a low stance. Doesn't seem like he really wants to fight, does it? He rarely moves to attack, and when he does strike, it's only a single swipe.

HP 53

JUNIOR MP (WITH SWORD)

This low-rank military officer swings twice consecutively with his long, thin blade. His ability to target Ed and Al is surprisingly poor (hence his low rank), so even if you are relatively close by, he may fail to attack. Take advantage of this delay to get in the first hit.

HP 60

TRAIN HIJACKER (ALCHEMIST)

This flame-manipulating alchemist wears a green hood. He is quite susceptible to normal attacks, but don't ignore his ability to summon bursts of fire. His HP and defense are the lowest in the entire hijacker group, so you should have no problem defeating him quickly with a couple of solid Lance blows.

HP 40

JUNIOR MP (WITH GUN)

This junior officer attacks with the handgun he carries. Usually he fires only one shot, but he may fire two at close range. In either case, the Junior MP will raise his right arm just before he fires, so it shouldn't be too hard to sidestep his attack.

HP 52

TRAIN HIJACKER (RIFLE)

This card-carrying member of the People's Eastern Revolution Front carries a small rifle and wears the group's signature blue bandana. His aim isn't very accurate, but you'll take quite a bit of damage if it hits, so keep on your toes.

HP 48

BOUNCER

A considerably stronger enemy, the Bouncer is the most powerful member of the train-jacking contingent. This grunt must have been handpicked by the rebel ringleader. His HP, defense, and attack power are all higher than the others' in the criminal group and the mechanical arms he uses to pummel his opponents contain awesome power.

However, since the Bouncer's brutal punch is his only attack you can easily dodge it if you watch his arms. Note that he leaves himself wide open to a counterattack right after he swings. Nail him then! His biggest weakness is his considerable lack of speed and painfully, slow turning rate. He's easy to beat if you concentrate on flanking him while he's setting up his attack.

HP 80

STAGE 2

AUTOMAIL PANTHER

Both front legs on this automail-strengthened big cat have been replaced with mechanical armored ones. Its reach is short, but its attack is brutal. The Panther is still a flesh-and-blood animal, vulnerable to bullets and fire. Alchemic defense is also a weak point, so attacking with a flame-imbued sword is also quite effective.

HP 200

BANDIT (RIFLE)

This Reminess Gorge bandit has traded in his sword for a rifle. Compared to the Train Hijacker, this guy moves around a lot and will both retreat and advance. He also shoots more often and fires faster projectiles than his train counterpart. If you weave enough, you can close in without getting hit. The best way to advance is to roll forward just as he raises his rifle to aim.

HP 130

BANDIT (WITH SWORD)

This redshirt bandit is based in Reminess Gorge. He typically performs two consecutive attacks, and if the first one connects, so will the second. Don't stand directly in front of him, and whatever you do, don't get hit by that first strike!

HP 140

BANDIT (ALCHEMIST)

The spear-slinging Bandit alchemist is easily distinguishable by his yellow hood. The stone-based alchemic arts he uses are very powerful, but his HP and defense are low. Get in close and take him out fast!

HP 115

WINGED SNAKE

A creature created by melding a snake with a bird, this odd chimera is annoyingly agile and fast. The Winged Snake has an extraordinarily high alchemic defense, so physical attacks will be your most effective weapon against it.

HP 130

GARGOYLE CHIMERA

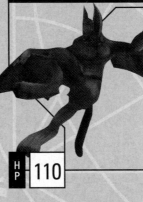

From the looks of the Gargoyle's powerful, well developed hind legs, it seems that this flying chimera was created by melding a dog, cat, or other four-legged animal with a bat. This bat creature can surprise you from behind, dropping suddenly from high places you cannot see. Once Gargoyles strike, use your onscreen radar map to keep an eye on their location. Your most effective counterattack is with a Crossbow or Gatling Gun, but be patient; Gargoyles can be difficult to target.

HP 110

GATOR-BOAR

This huge, savage beast lets out a ferocious roar as it charges forward. One strike won't do much damage, but be wary because this foe usually travels in packs. Its main weapon is its teeth, which snap at you twice in quick succession. But don't focus just on the Gator-Boar's head. Pay attention to the other end too. Its nasty tail-whip can knock you down, so watch out!

HP 200

SHELLFISH CHIMERA

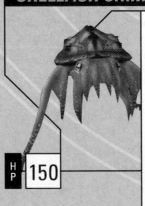

That's right; someone fused a crustacean with a squid. A living organism resembling an ammonite, the Shellfish sports a protective shell with an extremely high defense value. It whacks at you with tentacles, and its spinning charge attack is very damaging. However, it has low defense against alchemy, so if you slam down some Stonespikes in its face (if you can call what it has a "face"), you should have no problem defeating this creepy creature. It wouldn't be a bad idea to mix alchemy into your regular combos either.

HP 150

STAGE 3

GAME BASICS

COMBAT TACTICS

CHARACTERS

EQUIPMENT

ENEMIES

WALKTHROUGH

APPENDIX

GORILLA-GOAT

This supernatural fusion beast has the head of a goat and the body of a gorilla. The Gorilla-Goat now rules the ravaged streets of Hiessgart; its lumbering body is big enough to block a narrow city path. This beast features very high HP, defense, and attack power. Its weakness is a low alchemic defense, so be sure to attack with lots of alchemy. Transmuted Cannons are particularly effective.

HP **250**

THIEF (WITH SWORD)

This relentless town thief roams the Hiessgart wastelands. His attack is swift, and he'll slash diagonally at you twice. While thieves carrying guns sneak around, the ones wielding swords walk and run normally.

HP **150**

GATOR-BOAR LV.2

This creature's HP is the same as that of its cousins found in the Reminess canyon and caves. But its defense and attack power are increased, and its elemental resistances are different too. It is now weak to flame too, but Lightning-based attacks are still its biggest weakness.

HP **200**

SHELLFISH CHIMERA LV.2

A step up from the ugly shell-squids found in the cave, this version uses alchemy to create a flying bug-bomb that floats for a second then dive-bombs its target. One thing that hasn't changed is its weak alchemic defense, so you can defeat it safely if you attack it relentlessly with Stonespikes. Keep an eye on its two long tentacles. When the Shellfish raises them, it's about to zing you with three consecutive shots. Roll out of the way!

HP **180**

THIEF (RIFLE)

These sneaky thieves have claimed the ruins of Hiessgart sparse wastelands as their territory. Immediately recognizable from the tattoos on their back and arms, they like to sneak around silently and fire two shots at a time from the rifle they carry.

HP **150**

FLYING PUFFER

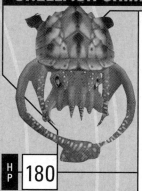

This dancing aerial blowfish floats in the air by flapping its tiny wings. It has low HP and doesn't move much, so it's fairly easy to hit. Defeat it with a simple combo, but watch out for its stinger tail, which can poison you. To avoid this try to attack the Flying Puffer from the side.

HP **100**

THIEF (ALCHEMIST)

When this bomb-transmuting alchemist raises his arms and the alchemy circle appears on his chest, a bomb suddenly appears and rolls towards you. It explodes soon after it stops rolling, so don't waste any time dodging away or you'll be caught in the blast!

HP **135**

KILLER FISH

This murderous flying fish thrives in shallow waters and jumps out to attack when approached. The Killer Fish is a small creature, but its large fangs give it a surprisingly high attack power. Don't underestimate this one!

HP **140**

ELECTRO-SLUG

Beware this chimera's paralyzing shock attack! This small, strangely colored creature seems to have been created from various insects. Its jump attack doesn't inflict much HP damage, but the electrical current it discharges will paralyze you instantly. Don't touch the Electro-Slug while it's discharging!

HP 120

STAGE 4

OUTLAW (SWORD)

This New Hiessgart vagabond looks pretty tough with his tattooed arms. He has no particularly distinguishing weak points or special attacks, so just be careful not to get hit when he swings his big sword twice in succession.

HP 250

OUTLAW (ALCHEMIST)

This New Hiessgart alchemist has the ability to summon stone pillars from the ground. This is a powerful skill, and just four hits can usually knock out Ed at this point. Avoid this attack at all costs!

HP 200

OUTLAW (RIFLE)

This outlaw has the same tattoos as his sword-wielding counterpart, and he carries a big rapid-fire rifle that makes the one used by the train bandits seem quaint. He can fire up to three successive shots at close range. At long range, he won't fire more than two.

HP 330

THUG (KNIFE)

The New Hiessgart Thug features an exceptionally high alchemic defense, but his normal defense is quite low. However, he makes up for it with a high success rate at blocking. Since he has roughly the same HP as other enemies, it takes a while to finish him off once he's started blocking. Fight him in a place where you can't be easily surrounded. This Thug's only attack is a slice with the blade in his right hand, so if you watch carefully you should be able to dodge. However, be wary of his astonishing jumping skills. He likes to make great leaps from far away, and it's not uncommon for him to suddenly appear behind you. Keep an eye on your radar.

HP 330

BOUNCER LV.2

A green-haired giant stylin' in a reddish, purple suit, the Lv. 2 version of the Bouncer has a frightening presence. A walking arsenal equipped with powerful arms, he boasts high HP and defense values, and he has the ability to block. More importantly, his hinged mechanical arms now open up to fire cannons! He's wide open just before he fires them, so dash up and hit him hard if you're close enough. The Bouncer is weak against arrows, cannonballs, and alchemy attacks.

HP 400

THUG (GUN)

The armed Thug exchanges half of his blocking rate for the ability to attack from range—one shot from long range, two shots when close. Most of his attributes are similar to those of the knife-wielding thug, but with his blocking rate reduced, so you should be able to defeat him quicker. This type of Thug does not have any particular elemental strengths or weaknesses, so attack him however you like.

340

BLAU

The youngest of the three Alchemy Brothers, Blau is skilled in ice-based alchemy. For whatever reason, his words can be heard by everyone except Ed and Al. A unique alchemist, Blau attacks with ice arrows and other piercing objects. He is a lifelong alchemist, so his alchemic defense is unusually high. Concentrate on normal strikes to defeat him.

H P 480

GAME BASICS

COMBAT TACTICS

CHARACTERS

EQUIPMENT

ENEMIES

WALKTHROUGH

APPENDIX

BANDIT LV.2 (SWORD)

This swordsman is somewhat stronger than others you encounter in the Hiessgart area. His HP, defense, and attack power are several times greater than the Lv. 1 version of Bandit.

300

ROT

The oldest of the three Alchemy brothers, Rot is skilled in flame alchemy. His distinguishing features are his red shirt and right eye patch. His best attack is to call forth a wall of fire directly before him. During close combat, this can be deadly Keep your distance if you see him summoning!

H P 530

BANDIT LV.2 (RIFLE)

Just like the Bandit Lv. 2 (Sword), this trigger-happy gunner has been powered up. Both his defense and gun power is several times greater than the Lv. 1 version.

270

GUY WITH CRANK

With his distinctive pink hood, this outlaw is easy to spot—which is good, because he has a gate crank you desperately need. His alchemic defense is high, but he isn't particularly strong in any one attribute, nor does he have any more HP than other stage enemies. If you equip a spear, sword, or dagger and attack continuously, he should fall quite easily.

H P 370

GARGOYLE CHIMERA LV.2

This chimera is a superior version of the standard Gargoyle creature. In addition to having its stats generally increased, it's now able to use alchemy and thus fling transmuted stone spears. However, since its claw slash is still its main attack, you won't see the alchemy attack too often.

330

STAGE 5

GATOR-BOAR LV.3

The reddish-purple, Lv. 3 version of the Gator-Boar has become a rather strong chimera. Its ability to use stone pillar alchemy (shooting a row of pillars from the ground) lets the beast attack from long range and makes up for its slow speed.

H P 350

ELECTRO-SLUG LV.2

The electric bug's color is not the only thing that's changed since you first discovered this creature on the lake's southern shore. It's been powered up all around. Don't get in too close and risk being paralyzed by his improved shock attack.

H P 200

AUTOMAIL PANTHER LV.2

This mechanical black panther boasts a noticeably improved attack. Unlike its spotted predecessor, which could only stand still and attack, this new panther can leap at its opponents.

H P 400

GORILLA-GOAT LV.2

This upgraded Gorilla-Goat can strike three powerful blows in a row and transmute a Cannon for a few shots. The blue monster has a lot of HP (640), plus a high defense and blocking rate, so use alchemy as your main weapon against it.

H P 640

WINGED SNAKE LV.2

At level 2, the flapping snake's standard attack now features two strikes. It has mastered some Wind alchemy, giving it the ability to create small tornados with itself at the center.

H P 280

MILITARY CRAB

The Military Crab combines high durability and defense with some new attack powers. It features the same "bubble breath" and rolling attacks that you faced in the Crab Chimera boss at the end of Stage 2, although it uses them infrequently. Its primary attack is a double-swipe with its massive pincer claws.

H P 600

GARGOYLE CHIMERA LV.3

This high-level bat creature can use stone-based alchemy and has all its stats powered up. He's not particularly weak or resistant to any one element, so fight him however you like. Flame or lightning based attacks are probably best because of their additional effects.

H P 240

CREEPING HODGEPODGE

This disgusting beast was created by mixing various types of several animals, although its two upside-down faces, protruding ribcage, and "hodgepodge" of legs leaves one unable to guess at what those animals were. It unleashes a sharp bone-slash that strikes from its back, plus an electrical shock attack. Finally, the creeper can use stone pillar alchemy.

H P 550

STAGE 6

GAME BASICS
COMBAT TACTICS
CHARACTERS
EQUIPMENT
ENEMIES
WALKTHROUGH
APPENDIX

JUNIOR STATE MP (SWORD)

This lower-ranked military police officer is still in training at Hiessgart Fortress. The Junior MP has no special abilities and is not particularly resistant against any one element. However, he is a well-balanced soldier.

HP 300

JUNIOR STATE MP (WITH GUN)

Just like his sword wielding counterpart, this gun-toting officer is well balanced. There's little visible difference between the Junior and Intermediate class versions of this enemy, so try to approach him from behind or the side, just in case.

HP 250

INTERMEDIATE STATE MP (SWORD)

This high-level standard officer works at the military headquarters located on the Hiessgart border. It's difficult to gain the upper hand against this well-balanced foe, as he's highly skilled across the board. Since his alchemic defense is higher than his standard defense, fight him with flame and lightning-imbued weapons.

HP 400

INTERMEDIATE STATE MP (GUN)

Just like his fellow swordsman officer, the Intermediate State MP armed with a pistol is a high-level, well-balanced soldier. He fires three bullets in quick succession at close range, so if you close in unprepared, you may very well meet an untimely demise. Always flank him to avoid getting caught by his three-shot attack.

HP 420

SENIOR STATE MP (SWORD)

This superior officer protects the military base with a patriotic fury. In addition to his three-strike slicing attack, he also has the uncanny ability to briefly transmute a Gatling Gun and fire a few rounds.

HP 480

SENIOR STATE MP (WITH GUN)

This first-rank military marksman attacks primarily with his handgun, firing four shots at long range, or two up close. Just like his sword-wielding counterpart, he can also transmute a Gatling Gun, making him a truly formidable foe.

HP 500

MP CHIEF (GUN)

This commanding officer raises the bar high. He has a stout resistance to elements, especially flame and lightning. His attacks feature a deadly 5-shot burst from his machine gun, plus he tosses grenades.

HP 550

TWO-HEADED DOG (JUNIOR)

This two-headed war dog roams the military base. Fast moving and vicious, this fusion beast likes to hunt you down. Hit it with any weapon.

HP 400

TANK

This small, but mighty, tank has high attributes—HP, attack power, defense, and alchemic defense. It also features high resistance to almost all elements. But its weakness is its lack of speed and a sluggish turning rate. If you stay vigilant, you can camp beside or behind it and hammer away as it turns with pathetic slowness trying to find you. (Our favorite anti-tank tactic: Spend a few minutes whacking at it with a Plastic Hammer, stringing together lots of long combos to earn fantastic EXP bonuses.)

HP 700

TWO-HEADED DOG (INTERMEDIATE)

This chimera upgrade has better stats than its junior pound mate. It moves quickly and aggressively and gives chase when it sees you. The intermediate two-headed dog also boasts an extraordinarily high alchemic defense, so be sure to use physical strikes when fighting it.

HP 450

MP CHIEF (WITH SWORD)

The top-ranked officer's HP, defense, and attack power are not as high as those of his gun-toting counterpart, but he is just as resistant to elemental attacks. He moves a bit slower than the other officers, so watch for the start of his attack, then quickly sidestep and counter.

HP 500

STAGE 7

TWO-HEADED DOG (SENIOR)

The strongest of the two-headed dogs features an extremely high alchemic defense, but its normal defense is low and it has no special resistance to elements. Beware its flame breath!

HP 550

UNDERGROUND BANDIT (ALCHEMIST)

A part of the same black-masked group, this fellow is the underground gang's alchemist. But his physical strikes are actually stronger than his alchemy, so don't underestimate them. Since he's susceptible to all elemental attacks, you can fight him however you like.

HP 380

UNDERGROUND BANDIT (WITH SWORD)

A member of the black-clad, mask-wearing bandit group that hangs in the Hiessgart waterways, the swordsman lashes out with three successive sword strikes when he attacks. He has strong resistance to all elements, so your best tactic is to cut him down with Stonespikes or standard weapons.

HP 410

UNDERGROUND BANDIT (GUN)

This masked bandit belongs to the group that uses the underground waterway as their base. He attacks with two shots up close and three from long range, and his accuracy is deadeye.

HP 410

SHELLFISH CHIMERA LV.3

The highest class shell-squid, it retains its three-hit attack and bomb transmutation ability. However, its alchemic defense is now incredibly high and its normal defense is weak. Finally, it's now capable of blocking your attacks, so be careful.

550

MERCENARY (KNIFE)

The Mercenary is the underground version of the Hit Man, with a high alchemic defense and low physical defense. However, his block rate has dropped and he attacks relentlessly. Watch out for the synthetic suction fans he transmutes! They trap you and leave you defenseless, so if he tries to use one, flee as fast as you can.

600

MERCENARY (GUN)

This mercenary boasts extremely high alchemy power and high alchemic defense. However, he attacks primarily with his handgun. His only resistance is to wind, so forget about equipping a weapon imbued with the Wind Element.

600

FEMALE KNIGHT

The attractive and deadly Female Knight makes her first appearance in the underground waterway's D block. She attacks with two swipes from the giant claw equipped on her right arm. Since her reach is long, be sure to keep your distance until you attack. You can damage her easily enough with standard strikes, just be aware that she is resistant to flame. The Female Knight also has the alchemic power to transmute a ball-and-chain onto your ankle, slowing you to a walk and rendering you temporarily defenseless.

700

ELECTRO-SLUG LV.3

Even though there is a higher-level slug in the sewers, this bug is actually the toughest of the Electro-Slugs. It retains its electrical charge and uses its water-cannon attack more frequently, making it dangerous even from afar.

H P **250**

ELECTRO-SLUG LV.4

This rare electric slug appears in diverging waterways. It often leaves behind a Reloader (Metal), and these items can be a great help when fighting the Sea Chimera later.

H P **400**

KILLER FISH LV.2

A stronger version of its vicious cousin that lives in shallow waters, this Lv. 2 fish still leaps out of the water to attack when prey draws near. Both its defense and attack power have been increased, and it now snaps at you several times in succession, lashing out with consecutive bites.

H P **350**

FLYING PUFFER LV.2

At level 2, this dancing blowfish is now red instead of yellow. However, it's still not very tough and dodges poorly when you are close enough to strike. All you have to worry about is the pink poison it releases when it self-destructs.

H P **310**

GAME BASICS

COMBAT TACTICS

CHARACTERS

EQUIPMENT

ENEMIES

WALKTHROUGH

APPENDIX

ARMORED KNIGHT

This entity is the same sort of transmutation as the Living Armor created by the Alchemy Brothers in New Hiessgart—except, this time around, it can *really* do some damage. It is after all a walking suit of armor, so it boasts a very high defense and attack power. However, the Armored Knight can't use alchemy at all, and you should be able to defeat it quickly as long as you stick to alchemy and long range attacks.

HP 800

MILITARY CRAB LV.2

The Lv. 2 version of crab doesn't have a specialized attack, but it is now capable of blocking *your* attacks, so be ready for a long fight. Its attack power is the most fearsome of the underground waterway, so be sure to dodge its strikes!

HP 600

STAGE 8

FEMALE KNIGHT LV.2

Both her arms are armored, but that right claw really stands out, doesn't it? This upgraded female knight will strike twice, and her blocking rate is considerably high, but she has little elemental resistance, so move in with a Lance or Sword imbued with an element.

HP 550

SENTRY (ALCHEMIST)

Like the Shellfish Chimera (Lv.2), this alchemist can assault Ed and Al with a transmuted floating bug-bomb. His alchemic ability is very high, so attack him before he attacks you. Any physical attack should do the job.

HP 470

FEMALE WARRIOR

In addition to wielding her cruel right claw, this warrior maiden brandishes a sword in her left hand. She can slice you to pieces with either. In fighting the Female Warrior, exploit her weaknesses to flame and the Steel Ball.

HP 570

BOUNCER LV.3

The strikes from this top-level Bouncer's armored mechanical arms are the strongest in the New Hiessgart Castle. In fact, this bodyguard's every strike can be lethal. He also fires two successive shots from his arm-cannon at long range.

HP 530

FEMALE WARRIOR LV.2

It's easy to mistake her for her weaker sister, the lower-level Female Warrior, but you can tell them apart by the weapons they carry. The upgraded Female Warrior is equipped with a spiked iron ball that deals devastating damage with each hit. Pay careful attention, because whether you choose to fight or avoid her, keeping a healthy distance is the key.

HP 530

SENTRY (MACHINE GUN)

The gun-toting imperial guard will fire his machine gun continuously from long range, and can also use alchemy to transmute a Gatling Gun. Dodge his shots as you move in and take him out at close range.

HP 500

HIT MAN (KNIFE)

This green-haired assassin possesses incredible jumping skills, and can leap long distances in the blink of an eye. Since he can block well at close range, too, the Hit Man is tough to beat.

480

HIT MAN (WITH GUN)

This assassin's secret suitcase hides a high-powered rifle, and he can also transmute suction fans to pull you into easy range. Just like his knife-wielding counterpart, he has amazing jumping ability, so keep your eye on him!

50

SENTRY (SWORD)

This grunting guard has a large arsenal of attacks. He throws grenades, transmutes and scatters bombs, and lashes out with his heavy sword. Since he has high HP and defense, you'll have to defeat him by exploiting his weaknesses: flames and cannon-fire. Take him out with explosives!

600

GATOR-BOAR LV.3

This highest grade of Gator-Boar is resistant to all elements. High HP is a given at level 3, but the Gator-Boar also possesses high defense, attack, and alchemic ability values. As if that wasn't bad enough, his successive strikes and stone pillar alchemy are extremely powerful. However, you can still perform a one-hit kill on him with a Katana sword. When in doubt, find a Katana!

600

WINGED SNAKE LV.3

Meet the fastest, highest grade of flying snake. Of course, this chimera's agility is incredible. The Lv. 3 Winged Snake can still conjure up a tornado, so back off when you see one coming.

530

GORILLA-GOAT LV.3

The highest grade Gorilla-Goat has incredible destructive power. This red version of the brawny beast boasts the highest stats of anything in the castle. Its huge claws and devastating cannon alchemy make it terribly powerful. Don't approach it unless you are prepared.

HP 630

ARMORED KNIGHT LV.2

Although the Lv. 2 Armored Knight isn't as strong as the level 3, it still features top-class defense and attack power. Watch out for its special charge attack and an alchemic burning blade that zips along the ground toward you. It isn't susceptible to any elements, so just take advantage of its greatest weakness; its lack of speed.

HP 700

ARMORED KNIGHT LV.3

Like its armored brothers, this warrior is ponderously slow of movement. But with 750 HP, the Lv. 3 Armored Knight is second only to the Lv. 2 Creeping Hodgepodge for overall durability. His attack power is high, and he possesses the special ability to deliver one-hit kills—so don't get hit even once!

HP 750

CREEPING HODGEPODGE LV.2

This freaky chimera has the highest HP and alchemic ability in the game—even higher then some of the bosses you fight! However, it's susceptible to things like lightning and poison, and is vulnerable to every element. Fight it however you like; just watch out for its nasty alchemic attacks.

HP 1500

GAME BASICS

COMBAT TACTICS

CHARACTERS

EQUIPMENT

ENEMIES

WALKTHROUGH

APPENDIX

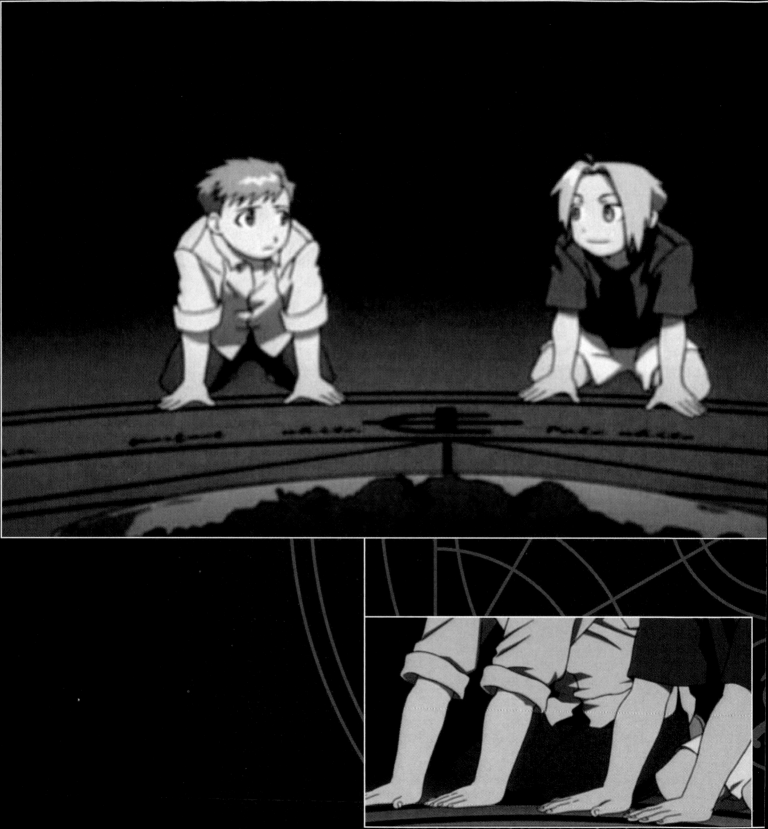

Fullmetal Alchemist and the Broken Angel continues the story of Edward Elric and his brother Alphonse. As the game opens, you get a recap of their situation:

Man gains nothing without sacrifice. To gain something, an equivalent price must be paid. This is alchemy's law of equivalent exchange.

Edward Elric. A young prodigy who became a State Alchemist at the age of 12. He is now 15 years old. His alias, "Fullmetal," derives from the fact that his right arm and left leg are metallic artificial limbs made from a material known as automail.

Alphonse Elric. Edward's younger brother. Inside the giant suit of armor lies the soul of a fourteen-year-old boy with a gentle heart. Only his soul occupies the suit of armor; he no longer has a physical body.

In their youth, the Elric brothers tried to revive their deceased mother through the powers of alchemy. The results were tragic. As the price for attempting the forbidden act, Ed lost his left leg. Al lost his entire body.

Ed sacrificed his right arm and succeeded in transmuting Al's soul, binding it into a nearby suit of armor. But their mother never came back, and the price they paid was far too great.

To regain their bodies and return all to its previous state, the Elric brothers started on a journey to find the legendary Philosopher's Stone …

CENTRAL RAILWAY

STAGE 1:
CENTRAL
RAILROAD

Coach Car

Train Rooftop

Freight Car 1

Freight Car 2

Coach Cars

Train Rooftop

First Class Car

Lounge Car

Military Man

Engine Rooftop

Colonel Genz
Bresslau

The first stage functions as a kind of tutorial, guiding the player through the basics of gameplay while fighting up the length of the Central-bound train. As the story opens, the Elrics and their guardian, Major Alex Louis Armstrong, sit brooding in a coach car. The train approaches the junction at Hiessgart—a city that, according to Alphonse, "brings back memories." The boys once visited an alchemist there named Wilhelm and his daughter Selene.

Suddenly, an explosion rattles the car. Hijackers calling themselves the People's Eastern Revolution Front announce they've taken control of the train, and two thugs burst into the coach car. Ed, Al, and Armstrong quickly dispose of the immediate threat and prepare to secure the train.

START: COACH CAR

After the cut-scene, you take control of Ed in Car 12. Al exits via the coach car's front door, while Major Armstrong takes up position down the aisle, blocking access to the train's rear.

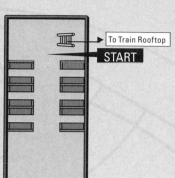

Review the movement and camera controls, then approach the ladder just ahead. Push the Left Analog Stick forward to climb the ladder to the train's roof.

To Train Rooftop

START

UP ONLY

Major Armstrong won't let Ed pass to the rear, and Ed won't exit via the car's front door. The only way out of the coach car is up the ladder.

TRAIN ROOFTOP

On top of the train, three Train Hijackers armed with swords await Ed. Here the game introduces the basics of attacking. Hop across to Car 11 and face the nearest enemy. Advance to close range and press the ● button to attack. Press the ● button repeatedly to create quick-strike combo attacks and add a deadly Accu-Strike at the end of the combo.

Occasionally, defeated enemies will drop item bags. Early in the game, the dropped bags contain only elixirs. Make sure you scoop up any of these spoils of victory.

After defeating all of the enemies, the game introduces the basics of alchemy, a useful skill for both defensive and offensive maneuvers. Use some alchemy on the next wave of Train Hijackers, then walk toward the front of the train and drop down through the opening in the roof.

To Freight Car

From Coach Car

BASIC ALCHEMY

Here's a quick review of Ed's two basic alchemy powers.

Defensive: Press the ● button to plant a Rockblocker on the ground in front of Ed. Rockblockers shield you from enemy attacks. You can also hop on top of Rockblockers, and use them as platforms to reach higher areas.

Offensive: Hold down the ● button, then release it to unleash Stonespikes from the ground in front of Ed.

GAME BASICS

COMBAT TACTICS

CHARACTERS

EQUIPMENT

ENEMIES

WALKTHROUGH

STAGE 1: CENTRAL RAILROAD

STAGE 2: REMINESS GORGE

STAGE 3: HIESSGART

STAGE 4: NEW HIESSGART, PART 1

STAGE 5: NEW HIESSGART, PART 2

STAGE 6: NEW HIESSGART CASTLE

STAGE 7: HIESSGART ARMY FORTRESS

STAGE 8: UNDERGROUND WATERWAY

APPENDIX

FREIGHT CAR 1

STAGE 1: CENTRAL RAILROAD

Coach Car
Train Rooftop
Freight Car 1
Freight Car 2
Coach Cars
Train Rooftop
First Class Car
Lounge Car
Military Man
Engine Rooftop
Colonel Genz Bresslau

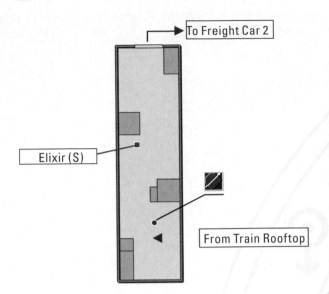

To Freight Car 2

Elixir (S)

From Train Rooftop

Inside the freight car, the game introduces Ed's ability to transmute objects into various weapons. See the briefcase on the floor? Hold down the ● button to view green circles surrounding the object and a weapon icon (a Lance) glowing above it. Walk inside the green circles, then release the button. This transmutes the briefcase into a Lance!

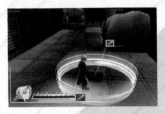

Equip the Lance by stepping close to it (an energy circle glows brightly beneath it on the floor) and press the ▲ button. The game explains how to perform combos using equipped weapons. (See the tip box on this page for a quick review.)

After equipping the Lance, two purple-clad Junior MPs armed with longswords enter the far end of the freight car. Attack them with nifty Lance combos by mixing up button presses of the ●, ◉, and ✖ buttons. After you defeat the foes, stand next to the treasure chest in the middle of the freight car and press the ● button to nab the **Elixir (S)** inside. Exit through the forward door.

COMBOS USING TRANSMUTED WEAPONS

Create combo strikes with a transmuted weapon whenever possible. Combos can be very powerful attacks—plus they look cool! Note that you can drop Stonespikes into a sequence of strikes by pressing the ● button during a combo attack.

Examples of Lance combos are as follows:

● → ◉ → ● → ●

● → ● → ◉ → ● → ●

● → ● → ◉ → ✖ → ●

With good timing, it is possible to follow Stonespikes with strikes, but keep in mind that you may risk missing your target.

FREIGHT CAR 2

In the next freight car, three sword-wielding Train Hijackers lurk at the far end of the car. Here you learn more about transmutable weapons. Certain objects can be transmuted into large mounted weapons that either Al or Ed can operate. Press and hold the ● button to activate Ed's Alchemy Gauge, then walk to the nearby beverage cart until he's inside the cart's Alchemy circles.

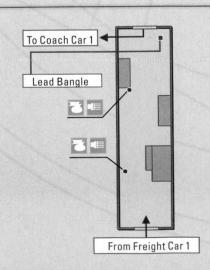

To Coach Car 1

Lead Bangle

From Freight Car 1

EYES ON THE ICON

Remember: When you hold down the ● button, step inside the beverage cart's Alchemy circles and release the button to make Ed transmute the cart into the weapon indicated by the icon that is highlighted above the cart. Do *not* release the button until you are sure the weapon you want is highlighted!

Different levels of the Alchemy Gauge provide a choice of two weapon types, indicated by the pair of icons that appear over the object. In this case, Ed can transmute the cart into either a lower-level weapon (a Cannon) when the Alchemy Gauge is blue, or a higher-level weapon (a Gatling Gun) when the gauge is red.

Cannon: To transmute the cart into the lower-level Cannon, press and hold the ● button and press the left directional button to highlight the Cannon icon (the one on the left). Then quickly release the ● button to create the Cannon.

Gatling Gun: To transmute the cart into the higher-level Gatling Gun, press and hold the ● button until the Alchemy Gauge fills up with red and the Gatling Gun icon (the one on the right) is highlighted. Release the ● button to create the Gatling Gun.

Walk inside the large weapon's glowing energy ring and press the ● button to mount the weapon. Press the ● button to fire the weapon and defeat the enemies inside the room. Press the ● button again to dismount.

While walking toward the car's exit door, two more Train Hijackers (one is a hooded alchemist) appear behind Ed. Transmute the other beverage cart near the front of the freight car and use it to defeat those enemies as well.

At this point, Ed should level up. When you level up, you not only restore full HP but you also receive *Bonus Points*. Use these points to increase Ed and Al's attributes in the Bonus Point section of the main menu. (For more on this, see the Bonus Points section in the "Getting Started" chapter.)

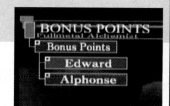

After distributing the Bonus Points, head toward the door and open the treasure chest in the corner to nab a nifty **Lead Bangle**. Go to the Menu screen again and select Accessories, then equip Ed with the new bangle to boost his ATK stat by 1. Return to the game and walk toward the door. Al rejoins Ed and the duo heads into the next train car.

COACH CAR 1

The coach car opens with a brief tutorial on giving commands to Al. Defeat the lone rifle-toting Train Hijacker, then take on any others who appear. Make sure you try Al's "Tackle" command a few times by pressing the R1 button when Ed faces an enemy.

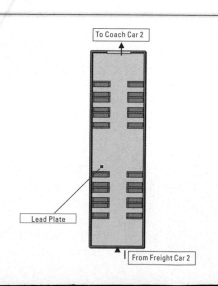

To Coach Car 2

Lead Plate

From Freight Car 2

GAME BASICS

COMBAT TACTICS

CHARACTERS

EQUIPMENT

ENEMIES

WALKTHROUGH

STAGE 1:
CENTRAL
RAILROAD

STAGE 2:
REMINESS GORGE

STAGE 3:
HIESSGART

STAGE 4:
NEW HIESSGART,
PART 1

STAGE 5:
NEW HIESSGART,
PART 2

STAGE 6:
NEW HIESSGART
CASTLE

STAGE 7:
HIESSGART ARMY
FORTRESS

STAGE 8:
UNDERGROUND
WATERWAY

APPENDIX

STAGE 1:
CENTRAL
RAILROAD

Coach Car
Train Rooftop
Freight Car 1
Freight Car 2
Coach Cars
Train Rooftop
First Class Car
Lounge Car
Military Man
Engine Rooftop
Colonel Genz
Bresslau

CLOSE RANGE

When fighting enemies with long-range weapons, quickly rush toward them to close the distance between the enemies and Ed.

Don't forget to open the treasure chest tucked behind the left row of seats for a **Lead Plate**. Equip it on Ed and defeat the three pistol-armed Junior MPs who enter next. Exit toward the front.

COACH CAR 2

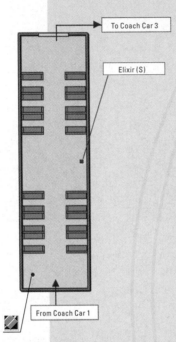

To Coach Car 3

Elixir (S)

From Coach Car 1

Defeat all the enemies that appear, including the tough Bouncer, and open the chest in the center of the car for another **Elixir (S)**. Exit toward the front.

In the next car, the game provides a tutorial on how to transmute weapons for Al. Transmute the nearby trash bin into a Lance for Al, then walk inside the Lance's energy ring and press the R1 button to make Al equip the weapon.

AL'S WEAPONS

Al fights more effectively with a weapon, of course. But remember that Al's weapons can be used only a limited number of times. (They disappear when expended.) Keep on the lookout for new weapons for Al! Hold down the ● button to fire up Ed's Alchemy Gauge each time you enter a new area and look for the blue or green weapon icons above transmutable objects.

COACH CAR 3

Inside the next car, defeat all of the enemies who drop from the ceiling hatch into the room. One good tactic is to transmute the beverage cart into a Gatling Gun, step inside its energy ring, and press the R1 button to make Al man the weapon. Then run Ed up the aisle to whack away with his Lance while Al guns them down. Note that a second transmutable cart is located near the front of the car if you need it.

After defeating all of the enemies, Ed and Al must part ways again. Before you proceed up the ladder to the roof, walk toward the front of the car and get the **Elixir (S)** in the chest hidden behind the left row of seats.

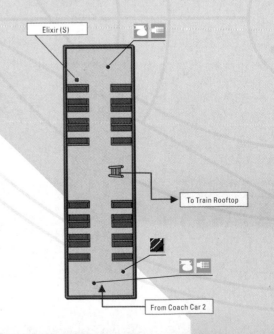

Elixir (S)

To Train Rooftop

From Coach Car 2

TRAIN ROOFTOP

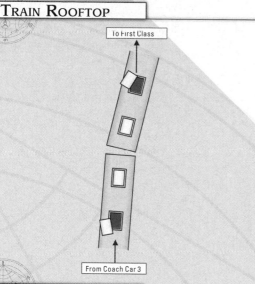

To First Class

From Coach Car 3

On the roof, the game provides two tutorials, one on dodge moves and the other on "breakfalling," both very useful maneuvers to master. Here the going is not so tough, however, so it's easy to practice the new maneuvers. Defeat all the enemies that appear and hop down through the open hatch up ahead.

FIRST CLASS

Walk to the front of the car to find a save point. Before you save, though, open the chest hidden behind the seats for an **Elixir (S)**. Also, look for another briefcase in the center of the car and transmute it into a Lance for Ed if he's without a weapon.

Approach the door next to the save point to trigger a cut-scene. Al warns that the leader of the hijackers must be up front. He also points out the military garb worn by some of the so-called "hijackers." Odd, isn't it?

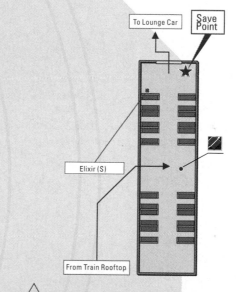

To Lounge Car

Save Point

Elixir (S)

From Train Rooftop

SAVE OFTEN!

Save your game *every time* you reach a save point. This not only preserves your progress, but it also restores full HP for both Ed and Al.

LOUNGE CAR

Inside the fancy lounge car, Ed and Al encounter an army officer—an elite military policeman, no less—who appears to be one of the ring leaders of the hijackers. After a short exchange with the Military Man, the game's first boss fight begins.

To Engine Rooftop

Save Point

BOSS

From First Class

GAME BASICS

COMBAT TACTICS

CHARACTERS

EQUIPMENT

ENEMIES

WALKTHROUGH

STAGE 1: CENTRAL RAILROAD

STAGE 2: REMINESS GORGE

STAGE 3: HIESSGART

STAGE 4: NEW HIESSGART, PART 1

STAGE 5: NEW HEISSGART, PART 2

STAGE 6: NEW HEISSGART CASTLE

STAGE 7: HIESSGART ARMY FORTRESS

STAGE 8: UNDERGROUND WATERWAY

APPENDIX

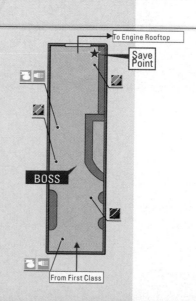

STAGE 1:
CENTRAL
RAILROAD

Coach Car
Train Rooftop
Freight Car 1
Freight Car 2
Coach Cars
Train Rooftop
First Class Car
Lounge Car
Military Man
Engine Rooftop
Colonel Genz
Bresslau

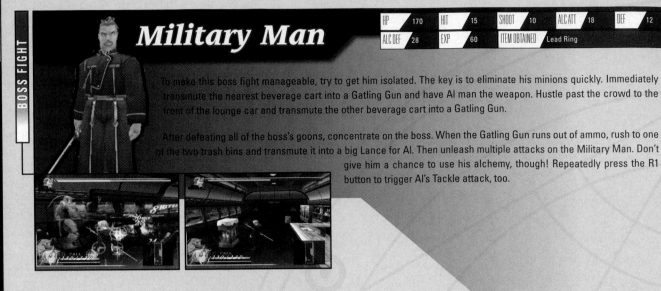

Military Man

| HP | 170 | HIT | 15 | SHOOT | 10 | ALC ATT | 18 | DEF | 12 |
| ALC DEF | 28 | EXP | 60 | ITEM OBTAINED | Lead Ring | | | | |

To make this boss fight manageable, try to get him isolated. The key is to eliminate his minions quickly. Immediately transmute the nearest beverage cart into a Gatling Gun and have Al man the weapon. Hustle past the crowd to the front of the lounge car and transmute the other beverage cart into a Gatling Gun.

After defeating all of the boss's goons, concentrate on the boss. When the Gatling Gun runs out of ammo, rush to one of the two trash bins and transmute it into a big Lance for Al. Then unleash multiple attacks on the Military Man. Don't give him a chance to use his alchemy, though! Repeatedly press the R1 button to trigger Al's Tackle attack, too.

After you defeat the Military Man, the fallen fellow explains how the hijackers are all ex-military alchemists bound for Hiessgart with their leader, Colonel Genz Bresslau. Alchemists from across the land are gathering there to establish a "self-government" of alchemists led by none other than Professor Wilhelm Eiselstein, one of the famed Ten Alchemists. The officer then unexpectedly escapes out the door.

Before giving chase, however, use the save point in the corner of the car to replenish any lost HP, as a *stronger* boss awaits upon exiting this car. Transmute another trash bin into a Lance for Al, then exit to encounter Genz on the top of the train.

ENGINE ROOFTOP

Sure, this guy is a "mohawked psycho" (as Ed puts it), but Genz Bresslau is also a senior colonel in the military police. Known as the Armor-Piercing Alchemist, Genz is a bit tougher than his lieutenant, as you might expect. But with the right tactics, he's not too difficult to defeat.

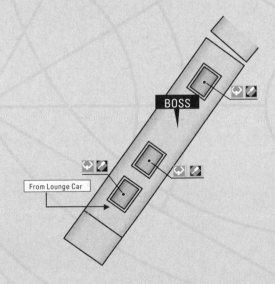

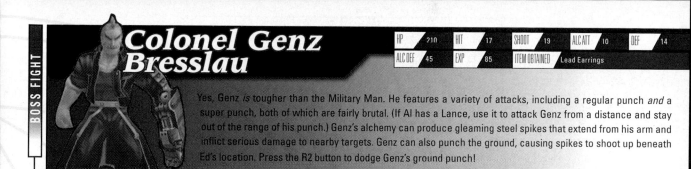

Colonel Genz Bresslau

HP	210	HIT	17	SHOOT	19	ALC ATT	10	DEF	14
ALC DEF	45	EXP	85	ITEM OBTAINED	Lead Earrings				

Yes, Genz *is* tougher than the Military Man. He features a variety of attacks, including a regular punch *and* a super punch, both of which are fairly brutal. (If Al has a Lance, use it to attack Genz from a distance and stay out of the range of his punch.) Genz's alchemy can produce gleaming steel spikes that extend from his arm and inflict serious damage to nearby targets. Genz can also punch the ground, causing spikes to shoot up beneath Ed's location. Press the R2 button to dodge Genz's ground punch!

Genz is a big jumper, so it can be somewhat difficult to trap him in a corner for an attack. Try this: Transmute the three roof domes into Steel Traps and lure Genz toward them. When he triggers a trap, Genz is momentarily immobilized, giving you a chance to unleash some attacks.

Attack using Ed's combos, but once you knock down Genz, quickly step away and wait for him to get up. If you stand over Genz as he rises, he will throw his arm and knock away anyone who is nearby. Repeat this process to make Genz fall in defeat.

GAME BASICS

COMBAT TACTICS

CHARACTERS

EQUIPMENT

ENEMIES

WALKTHROUGH

STAGE 1: CENTRAL RAILROAD

STAGE 2: REMINESS GORGE

STAGE 3: HIESSGART

STAGE 4: NEW HIESSGART, PART 1

STAGE 5: NEW HIESSGART, PART 2

STAGE 6: NEW HIESSGART CASTLE

STAGE 7: HIESSGART ARMY FORTRESS

STAGE 8: UNDERGROUND WATERWAY

APPENDIX

Despite this victory, Genz manages to enrage Ed with a comment about his stature. Ed's overreaction triggers a flaming train wreck, and thus this rail journey ends.

Tunnel

North Trestle

South Trestle

Mountain
Pass (South)

Mountain
Pass (North)

Caves

Crab Chimera

STAGE 2

REMINESS GORGE

This stage features railway trestles that are suspended over rugged terrain, dramatic cliffs and canyons, and a treacherous, underground labyrinth of mining tunnels and caverns. After the train wreck, Major Armstrong waits for Ed and Al near the collapsed tunnel entrance, but don't talk to him just yet. You can pick up a couple of items first.

BUMP UP YOUR STATS!

Don't forget to allocate the Bonus Points you earned by defeating the bosses in Stage 1. Go to the Menu screen and select Bonus Points, then distribute them to Ed and/or Al.

TUNNEL

Go past Armstrong to the opening in the fence on the left. (Don't get too close to the Major or you'll trigger the conversation! Hug the fence.) Drop down to a ledge below to find two treasure chests.

One chest contains a **Wind Element** and the other a **Lightning Element**. After picking up the items, climb the ladder back up to the tracks and approach Armstrong to make your report. The Major wants the boys to stay and help with the post-derailment recovery effort, but Ed has other ideas.

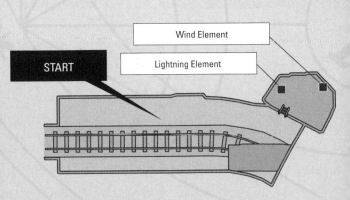

START

Wind Element

Lightning Element

NORTH TRESTLE

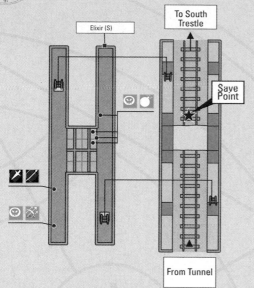

Elixir (S)

To South Trestle

Save Point

From Tunnel

The middle of the bridge has collapsed, so you can't follow the railroad tracks to the other side. Equip Ed with the Lead Earrings and, if you haven't already done so, equip Al with the Lead Ring. Find the nearby support pillar with a ladder (marked with a ladder icon) and climb up to the top.

Careful! Hostile foes and a disturbing flashback lurk above. Fortunately, there is a helpful tutorial on Special Attacks that Ed and Al can execute as a team. After the lesson, a special attack icon automatically appears. To use it, press and hold the ◉ button to fill Ed's Alchemy Gauge, move Ed close to Al or call Al closer, and when Al's command screen reads "Special," press the R1 button to execute the special attack. This should annihilate all of the enemies within the vicinity of this attack.

Run across the bridge to the pile of cinderblocks and transmute it into a Dagger or Lance for Ed. You can also transmute some of the nearby canisters and sacks into Bombs or Mines. Use these weapons to wipe out any remaining enemies and head toward the far end of the bridge. On one side is a treasure chest containing an **Elixir (S);** on the other side is a ladder opening. Climb down to get past the collapsed center of the bridge span. Use the save point to save your game, then continue across the bridge.

GAME BASICS

COMBAT TACTICS

CHARACTERS

EQUIPMENT

ENEMIES

WALKTHROUGH

STAGE 1: CENTRAL RAILROAD

STAGE 2: REMINESS GORGE

STAGE 3: HIESSGART

STAGE 4: NEW HIESSGART, PART 1

STAGE 5: NEW HIESSGART, PART 2

STAGE 6: NEW HIESSGART CASTLE

STAGE 7: HIESSGART ARMY FORTRESS

STAGE 8: UNDERGROUND WATERWAY

APPENDIX

SOUTH TRESTLE

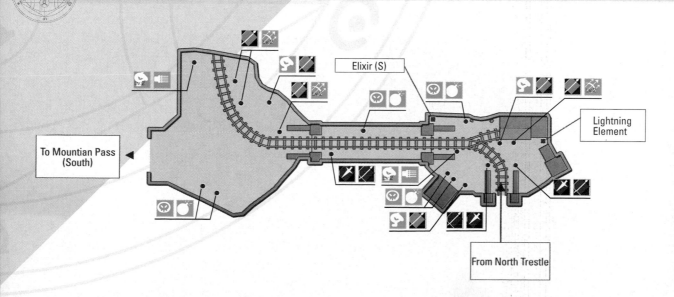

To Mountian Pass (South)

Elixir (S)

Lightning Element

From North Trestle

STAGE 2:
REMINESS GORGE

Tunnel
North Trestle
South Trestle
Mountain
Pass (South)
Mountain
Pass (North)
Caves
Crab Chimera

At the far end, a mob of Hijackers and Bandits refuse to let Ed and Al pass. Most of them have rifles that can inflict some serious damage. Before the fight, however, you see a short tutorial on the Fighting Frenzy state (which boosts your ATK and the amount of EXP points gained) and your Frenzy Special Attacks, which are similar to regular Special Attacks but more powerful. You start this battle with a Frenzy icon already available. Press and hold the ◉ button, lead Al to the center of the enemy group, then press the R1 button to activate the awesome Frenzy Special Attack.

BREAK THAT FALL!

One of the conditions that ends a Fighting Frenzy state is when Ed falls down—that is, he gets knocked to the ground by an enemy's attack. But you can avoid this by quickly pressing the ✖ button to activate a Breakfall maneuver. Ed pops right back to his feet and the Fighting Frenzy continues!

When the area is clear, Ed expresses interest in the old locomotive. Nab the **Lightning Element** from the chest in the eastern corner of the map. Also note the abundance of transmutable objects that can provide weapons for either Ed or Al. Head west toward the next bridge, and pick up the **Elixir (S)** in the chest hidden behind the strut to the right of the bridge entrance.

More Bandits prowl the bridge. Make your advance easier by transmuting the signal pole near the bridge entrance into a Gatling Gun. Hop aboard and carefully pick off the two distant thugs who pace into and out of sight. Then cross the bridge and eliminate the remaining Bandits.

CHARGE IT!

Here's a good place to apply a Lightning Element charge into your Lances. Press the ♠ button to drop the Lance, step into its energy ring, then hold down the ◉ button to fill Ed's Alchemy Gauge and see the Lightning icon. Release the button to zap the Lance with Lightning, then grab the weapon and proceed.

You can apply Lightning onto a weapon for Al, too. After you transmute a big Lance from a light pole, use the same technique described previously to charge the Lance before pressing the R1 button to order Al to use it.

Continue across the bridge. On the far side, a large group of Bandits await, including some pesky alchemists. Transmute a telephone pole into a Crossbow and let Al man it. (He's a very accurate shot.) Then transmute the nearby light pole into a Suction Machine and activate it (that is, step into its alchemy circle and press the ● button) to suck nearby enemies into an immobile cluster, giving Al some easy targets.

Once you clean out this area, transmute the other telephone poles into Crossbows (for later use) and walk toward the huge boulders that block the mountain pass to the west. This triggers a cut-scene; Ed decides to use the old locomotive to clear the pass. He transmutes the junker into a howitzer and blasts open the blocked passage.

Ed and Al end up next to the train/howitzer. Head back west across the bridge. Along the way, you see a Hijacker being chased along the tracks by a strange new enemy—a massive Gator-Boar chimera!

Continue across the span to find an entire *herd* of Gator-Boars. These beasts are very aggressive and have far more HP than any enemy you've previously encountered—200 HP, to be exact—and are more resistant to your attacks. To defeat them, assign Al to a previously transmuted Crossbow. (If you didn't transmute one yet, do so now!) When the area is clear, head west through the mountain pass.

GAME BASICS

COMBAT TACTICS

CHARACTERS

EQUIPMENT

ENEMIES

WALKTHROUGH

STAGE 1: CENTRAL RAILROAD

STAGE 2: REMINESS GORGE

STAGE 3: HIESSGART

STAGE 4: NEW HIESSGART, PART 1

STAGE 5: NEW HIESSGART, PART 2

STAGE 6: NEW HIESSGART CASTLE

STAGE 7: HIESSGART ARMY FORTRESS

STAGE 8: UNDERGROUND WATERWAY

APPENDIX

MOUNTAIN PASS (SOUTH)

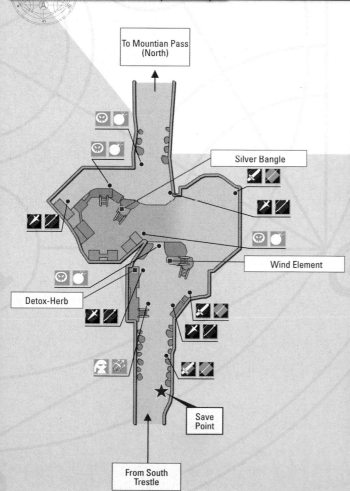

To Mountian Pass (North)

Silver Bangle

Wind Element

Detox-Herb

Save Point

From South Trestle

In the pass, Ed and Al discover a young girl climbing the canyon wall. As she reaches for a delicate, white flower growing from the rock face, the girl slips and falls. Ed involuntarily cushions her landing. After a short dialogue, Ed and Al give chase to the redheaded girl.

Save your game at the save point, then approach the nearby wooden wheelbarrow. You can transmute it into a big Sword for Al or a Katana that either brother can use. However, a katana works best against the next drooling horde of enemies.

STAGE 2:
REMINESS GORGE

Tunnel
North Trestle
South Trestle
Mountain
Pass (South)
Mountain
Pass (North)
Caves
Crab Chimera

Stepping into the open area triggers the arrival of a group of chimeras. The Katana can make short work of them since it randomly inflicts a one-hit kill. Even if you don't get the instant kill, a Katana strike still causes a tremendous amount of damage. Unfortunately, the Katana is only good for a few hits before it disappears. When it does so, transmute the second Katana from the object near the covered boxes. When that blade is expended, rely upon Stonespikes for attacking purposes. You can also transmute the nearby wooden box into a Crossbow and have Al man it.

WHAT A BOAR

Avoid getting surrounded by the Gator-Boar chimeras. They love to gang up on targets and inflict damage from behind.

Climb the ladder on the west side of the screen up to the top of the platform. Cross the planks onto the next platform and jump from the corner across the gap to another platform with a treasure chest. The chest contains a **Detox-Herb**.

MAKE A JUMP PLATFORM

If making the jump across the gap is too difficult, use alchemy to create a Rockblocker near the edge of the platform. Quickly walk Ed into the Rockblocker to hop on top—hurry before it crumbles!—and then try to jump across the gap again.

From this ledge, you can see another treasure chest on the other side of the cliff. Note the series of three platforms leading up the rock tower; the chest is on the second platform.

To reach it, jump down to ground level and head toward the rock tower. Approach the ladder that doesn't quite reach the ground. It's not possible to grab this ladder with a simple leap, so create a Rockblocker beneath it. Walk into the Rockblocker so Ed jumps on top, then hop up to snag a ladder rung. Climb up to the first platform. Repeat this process to grab the next ladder and climb to the middle platform. Acquire the **Wind Element** from the treasure chest.

Drop to the ground and go around the left (west) side of the rock tower. This leads to a ledge overlooking a gorge inhabited by Gargoyles and Automail Panthers. Transmute the pile of sacks into a Bomb and knock it into the gorge to damage a few enemies below. Then go around the other (east) side of the tower and follow the path leading down into the gorge. Along the way, transmute the mineral cart into another Katana for the looming battle. Wade into the assorted chimeras and wipe them out. Remember to use Ed's alchemy for Stonespikes attacks after the Katana is expended.

At the bottom of the gorge, a few more Gargoyles flap about. Knock them out of the air, finish them off, then climb the ladder to the platform. Follow the planks running across to more platforms on the left.

Use a Rockblocker as a jumping base when necessary to proceed higher up the cliffs until you reach a ledge that overlooks a ladder. Jump from the ledge's corner to reach the ladder and climb up to get the **Silver Bangle** from the chest. Equip Ed with this new accessory, replacing his old Lead Bangle.

From here, drop to the next platform below and leap across to the rock ledge. Finally, follow the path east into the next area. Watch out for Automail Panthers on the prowl!

JUMPING FROM ROCKBLOCKERS

Here's a good general tip for jumping puzzles in Fullmetal Alchemist. If a leap appears to be difficult, place a Rockblocker at the jump point. Walk Ed into the Rockblocker to get him on top of it, then jump before the Rockblocker crumbles. The added elevation makes jumping easier.

GAME BASICS

COMBAT TACTICS

CHARACTERS

EQUIPMENT

ENEMIES

WALKTHROUGH

STAGE 1: CENTRAL RAILROAD

STAGE 2: REMINESS GORGE

STAGE 3: HIESSGART

STAGE 4: NEW HIESSGART, PART 1

STAGE 5: NEW HIESSGART, PART 2

STAGE 6: NEW HIESSGART CASTLE

STAGE 7: HIESSGART ARMY FORTRESS

STAGE 8: UNDERGROUND WATERWAY

APPENDIX

MOUNTAIN PASS (NORTH)

This area features a large open canyon with various platforms, mineral carts, and high plank walkways. First things first: Drop down into the canyon itself and go chimera hunting before searching for the treasure chests on the various platforms. (Chances are you'll fall into the canyon a few times while hopping for treasure, so it's best to clear the ground floor first.) Transmute mineral carts into Katanas and give one to Al. Wipe out all the enemies on the canyon floor, then look for the two treasure chests on that level, one with a **Relax-Herb** and the other with a **Doubalixir (S).**

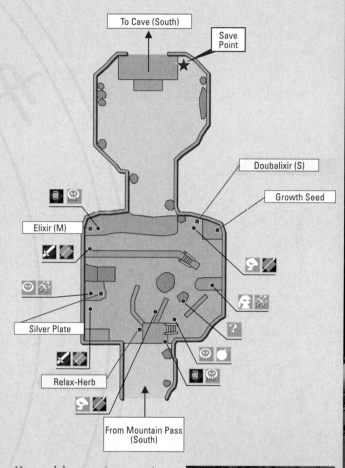

CROSSBOW RAIN

A tougher, alternate strategy in the north mountain pass is to immediately make the leap from the rightmost plank walkway to the crumbling rock column, then over to the ledge with the crate. Transmute the crate into a Crossbow and pick off chimeras below to the left.

Then hop down, hustle to the ladder, and climb back to the upper level. Now take the leftmost plank walkway and leap to the other ledge with the crate. Again, transmute that crate into a Crossbow and pick off the chimeras below.

To get the other chests, find the tall ladder and climb back to the upper platform. Walk carefully along the plank walkway to the left and follow it around the bend.

Use alchemy to create a Rockblocker halfway between the corner and the end of the plank path. Stand on top of the Rockblocker and jump across to the ledge with the wood crate and open the chest containing the **Silver Plate**. Equip Al with this new plate, replacing his old Lead Plate.

Hop down to the canyon floor and return to the ladder, climbing back to the upper platform. Now follow the plank walkway on the right. Walk all the way to the plank's end and jump across to the top of the tall rock column. (You may want to place a Rockblocker at the end of the plank first and jump from that.)

Don't linger atop the column! It will crumble shortly after you land on it. Ignore the thin row of planks to the right and jump straight across to the rock ledge with a wood crate. (The crate can be transmuted into a Crossbow.)

Now walk to the end of the plank walkway and jump north to the ledge with the torch. Open the treasure chest there to score an **Elixir (M)** and proceed east across the last planks and platforms, then north through the final pass.

STAGE 2:
REMINESS GORGE

Tunnel
North Trestle
South Trestle
Mountain
Pass (South)
Mountain
Pass (North)
Caves
Crab Chimera

FALLEN ED

If the rock column crumbles and Ed drops to the canyon floor without reaching the next ledge, it initially appears that your jumping route to the far wall of the canyon is gone. But don't worry. On the floor, just approach the fallen column's rock pile and use Ed's alchemy to rebuild it. Then climb the ladder and try the jump again.

If you have some spare time and want a laugh, deliberately fall off the column a bunch of times and witness Ed's frustration!

The boys catch a glimpse of the redheaded girl running into a monumental cave entrance up ahead. Use the save point just to the right of the entrance, then head directly into the depths.

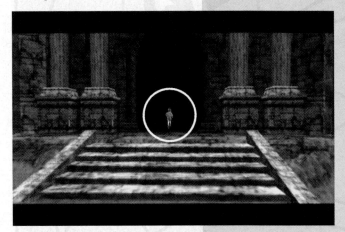

From the rock ledge, jump across to the green platform and climb the ladder to the second level, another plank walkway. On the second level, turn around and face the platform in the canyon's

northeast corner. Make a Rockblocker and jump over to nab the **Growth Seed** in the chest. Jump back to the green platform and climb the ladder again.

THE CAVES

This area features a series of connected underground caverns filled with creepy-crawly chimeras.

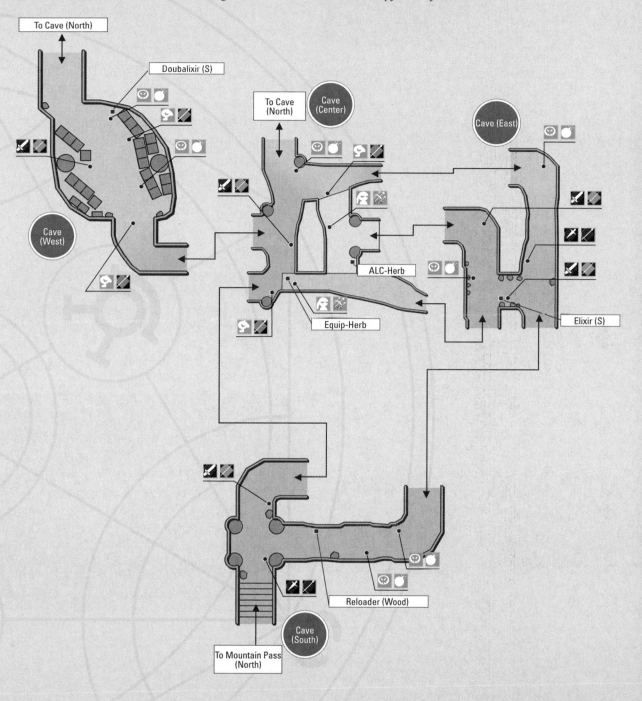

To Cave (North)

Doubalixir (S)

To Cave (North)

Cave (Center)

Cave (East)

Cave (West)

ALC-Herb

Equip-Herb

Elixir (S)

Reloader (Wood)

Cave (South)

To Mountain Pass (North)

GAME BASICS

COMBAT TACTICS

CHARACTERS

EQUIPMENT

ENEMIES

WALKTHROUGH

STAGE 1: CENTRAL RAILROAD

STAGE 2: REMINESS GORGE

STAGE 3: HIESSGART

STAGE 4: NEW HIESSGART, PART 1

STAGE 5: NEW HIESSGART, PART 2

STAGE 6: NEW HIESSGART CASTLE

STAGE 7: HIESSGART ARMY FORTRESS

STAGE 8: UNDERGROUND WATERWAY

APPENDIX

Cave (South)

Uh oh! A pair of Automail Panthers and a snarling Gator-Boar patrol the tunnel just up ahead. Note also the cinder blocks (Dagger or Lance for Ed) and the mineral cart (Sword for Al, Katana for either Ed or Al) are ready to be transmuted in the hall.

Defeat the beastly enemies and take the first right heading east down the long corridor. Watch out for more Gator-Boars appearing in the tunnel. Transmute the basket and sacks into Mines, then use a nice Special Attack to thin the porcine ranks. When the tunnel is clear, open the chest on the floor for a **Reloader (Wood)** and proceed to the end of the corridor.

STAGE 2:
REMINESS GORGE

Tunnel
North Trestle
South Trestle
Mountain
Pass (South)
Mountain
Pass (North)
Caves
Crab Chimera

Cave (East)

This room is shaped like an "H," with exits at each point. You enter the southeast corner of the room. Several Shellfish chimeras (a bizarre turtle/squid hybrid) waddle around this room. Watch  out for their spinning shell attack! It comes fast, so be ready to move the left analog stick to the right or left and press the R2 button to dive out of the way.

 These creepy creatures are very resistant to regular attacks, so transmute a Katana from the mineral cart just around the corner to the left and equip either Ed or Al with it. Its one-hit kill proves useful against the vicious shell-heads. After you defeat the chimeras in this area, open the chest in the middle of the room to nab an **Elixir (S)** and exit via the west passage.

Cave (Center)

The west exit leads to the highest ledge in this center cave area. Upon entering it, you will likely come under fire from a rifle-toting Bandit. Eliminate him, then transmute the nearby wooden crate into a Crossbow (Lv. 2) and order Al to man it. He'll extinguish quite a few enemies, including several down below.

Note: Don't jump down from the north end of the ledge! If you do, you'll end up in the lower level of the room and you'll be forced to find your way back up to the ledge via previously traveled caves if you want to fully explore this room. Instead, take a few steps south down the slope and open the chest for an **ALC-Herb**. Then drop down onto the mid-level from the south end of the ledge.

Head west to the wood crate, transmute it into a Crossbow, and let Al open fire with it. Open the nearby chest for an **Equip-Herb**. Now jump down to the bottom level and finish off  any Bandits or Gargoyle chimeras flapping about.

For a good frame of reference, there are six exits in this room:

- The northern exit leads to a dead end in Cave (North).

- The three exits on the east side all lead back to Cave (East); however, once you're at the bottom level of the room you can't exit from the southern two exits on the east side. Return to Cave (East) via the northeast exit.

- The southwest exit takes you back to the only other entrance in Cave (South). If you get lost in the caves, return to this room as your point of reference. You can start over to find all the chests or if you just want to fight enemies for EXP to level up.

- When you want to proceed, take the west exit to reach the next part of the caves.

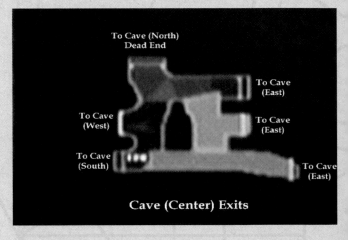

Cave (Center) Exits

Cave (West)

Get ready! As soon as you reach the center of this room, an infestation of Winged-Snake chimeras drops from the ceiling. A Special Attack (especially if Fighting Frenzy is active) can work wonders in this room, but expect more chimeras to appear. After defeating all of the chimeras in this room, get the **Doubalixir (S)** in the chest near the north end of the cave and continue north along the tunnel.

Cave (North)

Fight to the north through the Automail Panther and Gator-Boar chimeras pacing the corridor. Skip the first right turn; it leads east to a dead end; instead, continue north uphill and around the curve and veer right, entering an alcove to find a hidden chest containing an **Elixir (S).** Exit the alcove and turn right, climbing the slope until you reach a railroad crossing sign at the edge of a drop.

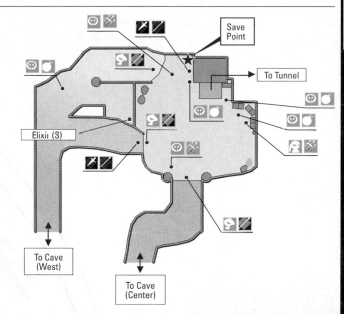

Drop down into the large open area with a save point tucked in the corner to the north. It's a good idea to save at this point, but before you do, transmute the nearby wooden crate into a large crossbow. Now transmute the Crossbow into Grenades, which will come in handy for the next boss fight.

Arm Ed with the Grenades, save your game, and hop onto the lift. When Ed is next to the lift control panel (indicated rather unsubtly by the pointing yellow arrow), press the ◉ button to ride up to the next level.

GAME BASICS

COMBAT TACTICS

CHARACTERS

EQUIPMENT

ENEMIES

WALKTHROUGH

STAGE 1: CENTRAL RAILROAD

STAGE 2: REMINESS GORGE

STAGE 3: HIESSGART

STAGE 4: NEW HIESSGART, PART 1

STAGE 5: NEW HIESSGART, PART 2

STAGE 6: NEW HIESSGART CASTLE

STAGE 7: HIESSGART ARMY FORTRESS

STAGE 8: UNDERGROUND WATERWAY

APPENDIX

Tunnel

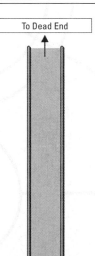

Suddenly, a colossal Crab Chimera drops behind the Elric boys. The objective here is to simply *run like crazy.* After the cut-scene, be prepared to sprint away from the crab down the length of the tunnel.

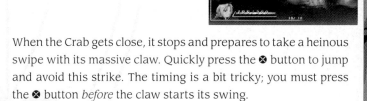

When the Crab gets close, it stops and prepares to take a heinous swipe with its massive claw. Quickly press the ❸ button to jump and avoid this strike. The timing is a bit tricky; you must press the ❸ button *before* the claw starts its swing.

Keep running down the tunnel and repeat this process each time the Crab Chimera gets close. Occasionally, the beast stops to spit poisonous bubbles. Fortunately, it shoots them in a stream from left to right so you can easily avoid them.

At the end of the tunnel, the big crab knocks Ed and Al unceremoniously down a hole into a giant cavern where the real boss fight begins.

STAGE 2:
REMINESS GORGE

Tunnel
North Trestle
South Trestle
Mountain
Pass (South)
Mountain
Pass (North)
Caves
Crab Chimera

This watery cavern is a trap—there's no way out! But when the Crab Chimera lands, wriggling on its back for a few seconds, Ed notes that its belly seems vulnerable. Hint, hint...

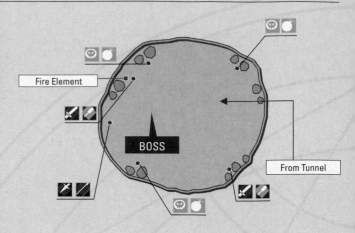

Fire Element

BOSS

From Tunnel

Crab Chimera

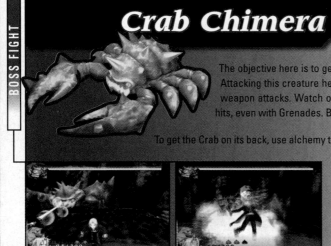

BOSS FIGHT

HP	600	HIT	30	SHOOT	28	ALC ATT	w25	DEF	23
ALC DEF	52	EXP	300	ITEM OBTAINED		Armlet of Accuracy			

The objective here is to get the Crab Chimera on its back so that its vulnerable underside is exposed. Attacking this creature head on is essentially useless, as its shell is nearly impervious to any of Ed's weapon attacks. Watch out for the boss's rolling attack, which makes it invulnerable to any of your hits, even with Grenades. Beware the creature's bubble attack, too!

To get the Crab on its back, use alchemy to ram a few Stonespikes in its face. Al's "Tackle" attack can knock over the bristly beast, too. As soon as the Crab goes belly up, toss some Grenades at it, one after another.

The monster should fall in defeat before it gets a chance to right itself. (If you ignored the previous suggestions and don't *have* any Grenades, you can transmute the nearby steel drums into Grenades.) There is also a **Fire Element** item inside a chest behind one of the steel drums. Pick it up before you defeat the boss.

After the fight, the boys wonder who could be conjuring up so many chimeras, and why. They also wonder what became of the redheaded girl. How could she have escaped all these monsters? Then we cut to Major Armstrong, who speaks via phone with someone he calls "Colonel."

When this Colonel learns that the Elric brothers are well on their way to Hiessgart, he blows a fuse and announces his plans to go to the town himself. Lastly, he mentions that one of his subordinates is already undercover in Hiessgart. He plans to have "her" look after the Elric brothers for now...

STAGE 3
HIESSGART

Welcome to Hiessgart, home of the ugliest hybrid chimeras you'll ever see. The place is a ghost town, and many large angry creatures lumber around the central plaza. It's time to look for the professor's house.

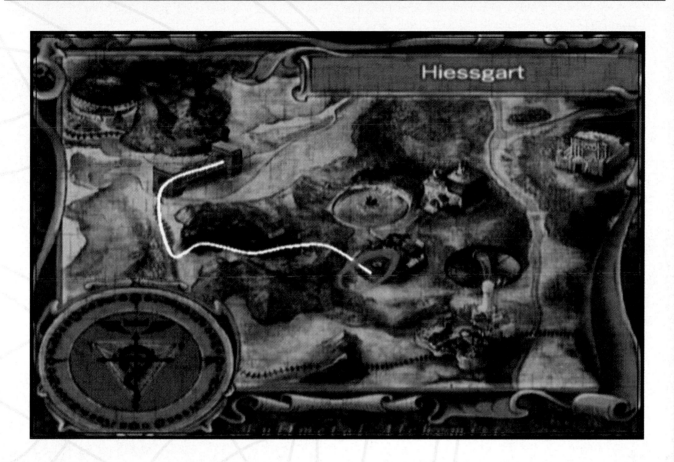

GAME BASICS

COMBAT TACTICS

CHARACTERS

EQUIPMENT

ENEMIES

WALKTHROUGH

STAGE 1:
CENTRAL
RAILROAD

STAGE 2:
REMINESS GORGE

STAGE 3:
HIESSGART

STAGE 4:
NEW HIESSGART,
PART 1

STAGE 5:
NEW HIESSGART,
PART 2

STAGE 6:
NEW HIESSGART
CASTLE

STAGE 7:
HIESSGART ARMY
FORTRESS

STAGE 8:
UNDERGROUND
WATERWAY

APPENDIX

CENTRAL PLAZA

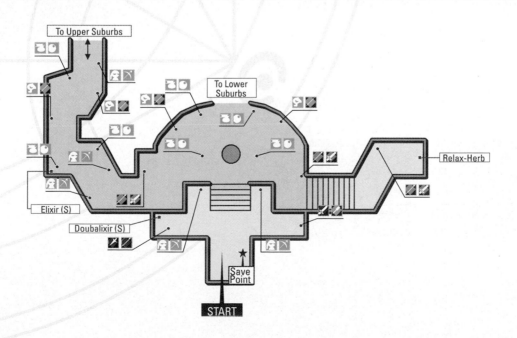

STAGE 3:
HIESSGART

Central Plaza
Upper Suburbs
Central Plaza
Lower Suburbs
Wastelands
Lakeside (South)
Lakeside (North)
Graveyard
Chapel
Masked Chimera

Down in the plaza, the archway to the Lower Suburbs (where the professor's house is located) is blocked by a raging inferno, so you'll have to find a way to put out the fire. Look for the save point to the east of Ed's starting position. Remember this when the going gets tough! Indeed, some enemies in this area are considerably tougher than any you've faced before.

SAVE YOUR GAME... AND YOUR ELIXIRS!

When you use a save point, both Ed and Al restore their full HP. Take advantage of this in Hiessgart Central Plaza. When their health gets low during combat, use the save point near the city gate to restore vitality instead of consuming valuable elixirs.

Walk to the west side of the upper plaza to find a chest containing a **Doubalixir (S).** You'll also find a Gator-Boar and a Gargoyle licking their chops. Run to the bench overlooking the plaza and transmute it into a Crossbow. Order Al onto the big gun and let him clear the area. Repeat this tactic on the east side of the upper plaza, again letting Al wipe out foes from his Crossbow perch. When he's done, transmute the nearby flower box into a set of Grenades for Al.

THE NEW BOAR

The Gator-Boar in Hiessgart is a different breed. Unlike this creature's lumbering predecessors back in the caves, the Lv. 2 version has a lightning fast charge attack and a nasty tail whip.

Head downstairs to tangle with the enormous Gorilla-Goat chimeras. Each monster features a painful triple-punch combo and a powerful ground-pound attack. Fortunately, good weapons are plentiful in the square. Transmute the light poles into Cannons (low-level alchemy) and slam cannonballs into those big critters

The map here splits into two sections. The path to the east leads to a dead end with a chest containing a **Relax-Herb**. Get that item first and then walk over to the flaming archway in the main plaza for a clue to putting out the flames.

A MORE PERSONAL BOW

You can transmute a Crossbow into a handheld bow for Ed that shoots explosive arrows. To aim and fire, hold down the ● button to go into first-person view. Move the Left Analog Stick to aim, then release the ● button to fire.

Head down the western path, but beware of the Gator-Boars roaming the area. Fortunately, plenty of metal drums line the streets, ready for transmutation into the deadly Katana blade. Along the way, pick up an **Elixir (S)** in the chest at the corner of the first bend, then proceed to the next area.

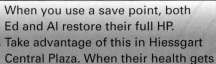

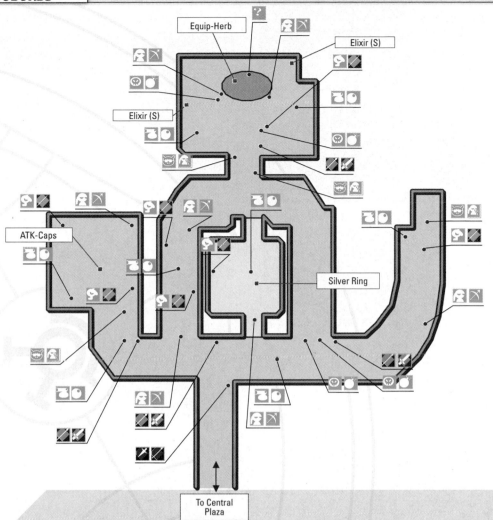

Equip-Herb

Elixir (S)

Elixir (S)

ATK-Caps

Silver Ring

To Central
Plaza

GAME BASICS

COMBAT TACTICS

CHARACTERS

EQUIPMENT

ENEMIES

WALKTHROUGH

STAGE 1:
CENTRAL
RAILROAD

STAGE 2:
REMINESS GORGE

STAGE 3:
HIESSGART

STAGE 4:
NEW HIESSGART,
PART 1

STAGE 5:
NEW HIESSGART,
PART 2

STAGE 6:
NEW HIESSGART
CASTLE

STAGE 7:
HIESSGART ARMY
FORTRESS

STAGE 8:
UNDERGROUND
WATERWAY

APPENDIX

Again, the map here has an east and west wing. The path up the middle features a big loop that meets at a construction site to the north where you'll find something of interest. But  first, turn left and follow the western side street. It leads into a dead-end square with an **ATK-Caps**, but as you approach, two big Gorilla-Goats appear. Transmute the light pole at the square's entrance and let Al blast the beasts with Cannon fire. (You can also transmute a "dummy" Ed, if you want to draw away enemy attention.)

 The path up the eastern side street leads to nothing but monsters, so unless you want to be thorough about clearing the map, you can avoid that path altogether. If you do head east, transmute a Crossbow and let Al use it to wipe out the Gator-Boars.

Now fight around the central loop to the construction zone in the north. Tough enemies block the route, but transmute Cannons and Crossbows for extra firepower. Once you reach your destination, approach the broken water pipe to see a brief cut-scene. But before you fix the broken water pipe, run around the area and transmute all objects in the area into large weapons (Cannons, Crossbows, Mines) for quick access. Then open the three chests in the area for two **Elixirs (S)** and one **Equip Herb**.

STAGE 3:
HIESSGART

Central Plaza
Upper Suburbs
Central Plaza
Lower Suburbs
Wastelands
Lakeside (South)
Lakeside (North)
Graveyard
Chapel
Masked Chimera

Now get ready for a wild fight! Fix the water pipe with Ed's alchemy; just hold down the ● button and approach the broken section, then release the button. Upon doing so, a swarm of enemies appear!

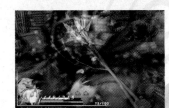

Surviving here is no small task, especially if the monsters surround Ed and Al, so keep an eye on their HP and consume Elixirs when necessary. Get Al to mount the various big guns you transmuted earlier—he's a deadeye gunner.

As you exit the construction area, note the low platform between buildings across the street directly ahead. It leads to a hidden courtyard. Walk up beneath the platform and create a Rockblocker, then climb up and jump onto the platform.

Walk to the courtyard in the middle. There's a **Silver Ring** inside a treasure chest, but opening the chest triggers a visit by four Gorilla-Goats, and fighting them in such a cramped area can be difficult. Before you approach the chest, transmute the lamppost into a Cannon and have Al mount it; transmute the rail into a Crossbow, too. Then open the chest and fight off the attackers. When finished, equip Al with the Silver Ring (replacing his Lead Ring). Exit south and return to Central Plaza.

CENTRAL PLAZA

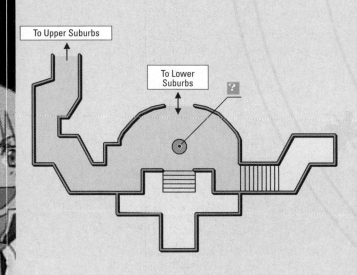

To Upper Suburbs

To Lower Suburbs

Back in Central Plaza, the fountain is flowing again. Unfortunately, the plaza is crawling with chimeras again, too. Remember, there's a save point near the main city gate, so wade into the monsters and wipe them out for the EXP. After the massacre, go save your game to heal up.

Approach the fountain and transmute it into a "super fire hydrant" to put out the fire, then proceed through the now-clear archway into the next area.

LOWER SUBURBS

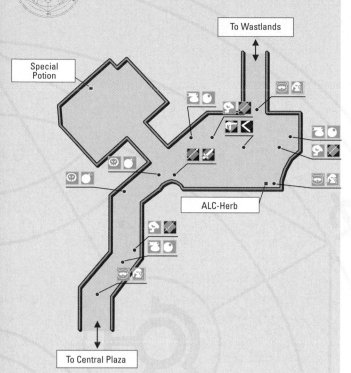

Special Potion

To Wastlands

ALC-Herb

To Central Plaza

Head down the crooked alley and destroy the Gator-Boars. When you reach the open area, numerous Gargoyles and Gorilla-Goats roam the area. Transmute a few weapons to help clear the chimeras, including a Boomerang that you can transmute a second time to make a Razor Ring, then add a Wind Element. The chest in the southeast corner contains an **ALC-Herb**.

Veer northwest into the little square plaza next. In a brief cut-scene, Ed recalls this as the location of Professor Eiselstein's house. After the cut-scene, defeat the enemies that appear and open the chest for a **Special Potion**. Return to the open area and exit the Lower Suburbs via the north passage.

GAME BASICS

COMBAT TACTICS

CHARACTERS

EQUIPMENT

ENEMIES

WALKTHROUGH

STAGE 1:
CENTRAL
RAILROAD

STAGE 2:
REMINESS GORGE

STAGE 3:
HIESSGART

STAGE 4:
NEW HIESSGART,
PART 1

STAGE 5:
NEW HIESSGART,
PART 2

STAGE 6:
NEW HIESSGART
CASTLE

STAGE 7:
HIESSGART ARMY
FORTRESS

STAGE 8:
UNDERGROUND
WATERWAY

APPENDIX

SUCK IT UP

Note that you can transmute a Suction Machine in the center of the area. Activate it to draw all enemies over to one location for some easy hits. Enemies are rendered largely helpless while being "suctioned."

WASTELANDS

Here, Thieves are as thick as, well, thieves. Some have rifles that can hit Ed from a distance. Step out into the first intersection and lure a crowd close together, then unleash a Special Attack in their midst. A number of Thieves will survive, however, so run to the east end of the lane and transmute the row of barricades into Mines.

Proceed north across the bridge and wipe out the next group of Thieves, including a bunch of hooded alchemists. Nab the **Elixir (S)** from the chest in the corner, then go west across the next bridge to face yet another den of Thieves. Look south for the chest with a **Reloader (Wood)** item. Find the nearby opening in the fence and drop down to the river level. Note that a ladder runs up the wall here.

STAGE 3: HIESSGART

Central Plaza
Upper Suburbs
Central Plaza
Lower Suburbs
Wastelands
Lakeside (South)
Lakeside (North)
Graveyard
Chapel
Masked Chimera

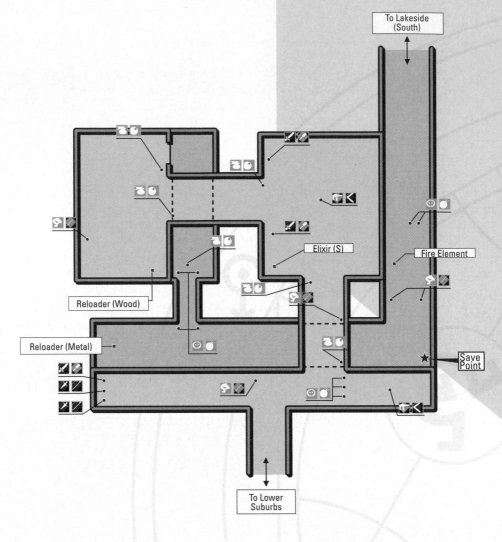

To Lakeside (South)

Elixir (S)

Fire Element

Reloader (Wood)

Reloader (Metal)

Save Point

To Lower Suburbs

Proceed south through the tunnel toward the narrow wooden bridge guarded by a single Thief. Careful, it's an ambush! The moment you eliminate the guard, a platoon of Thieves drops onto the bridge. Quickly fill Ed's Alchemy Gauge and unleash a Special Attack, if you have any left.

On the other side, turn right (west) and find the chest at the dead end for a **Reloader (Metal)** item. Go due east now, underneath the bridge, and save your game at the save point. Find a **Fire Element** item in the chest a short distance to the north. Nail the last two Thief-Alchemists and continue north to the area exit.

LAKESIDE (SOUTH)

At first glance, the lakeside area appears daunting. A *lot* of hostile creatures are creeping, crawling and hovering over the lawn—Flying Puffers, Electro-Slugs, and the powerful Shellfish chimeras. Fortunately, many objects here are transmutable into weapons, making the fight considerably easier. Special Attacks always work well in a swarm of enemies, too. Turn trees into Quintuple Crossbows and let Al use them to decimate enemies.

When you're done, look for a **Reloader (Metal)** item in a chest behind one of the broken pillars and another **Reloader (Metal)** as you exit the area to the north.

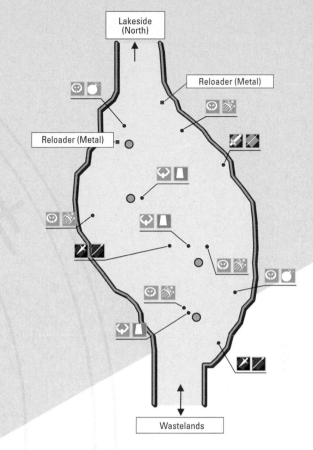

Lakeside (North)

Reloader (Metal)

Reloader (Metal)

Wastelands

USE TRAPS

Transmute Mines and Steel Traps and lure monsters over them to inflict heavy damage. You can also make heavy stone Monoliths to knock over on top of attackers.

GAME BASICS

COMBAT TACTICS

CHARACTERS

EQUIPMENT

ENEMIES

WALKTHROUGH

STAGE 1: CENTRAL RAILROAD

STAGE 2: REMINESS GORGE

STAGE 3: HIESSGART

STAGE 4: NEW HIESSGART, PART 1

STAGE 5: NEW HIESSGART, PART 2

STAGE 6: NEW HIESSGART CASTLE

STAGE 7: HIESSGART ARMY FORTRESS

STAGE 8: UNDERGROUND WATERWAY

APPENDIX

LAKESIDE (NORTH)

A stream infested with pests runs through the middle of this map. In the area south of the waterfall, find a chest containing an **ALC-Herb**. As you approach the stream, Ed spots the silhouette of the redheaded "brat" running north. Transmute the tree into a Quintuple Crossbow to help clear the waters, then hop in to find a **Reloader (Metal)** chest at the mouth of the stream and an **Elixir (S)** chest beneath the waterfall.

Central Plaza

Upper Suburbs

Central Plaza

Lower Suburbs

Wastelands

Lakeside (South)

Lakeside (North)

Graveyard

Chapel

Masked Chimera

In the area north of the stream, look for a **Relax-Herb** in the chest between the broken columns and a **Reloader (Metal)** in the northwest corner on the upper level. Head up the slope and into the next area.

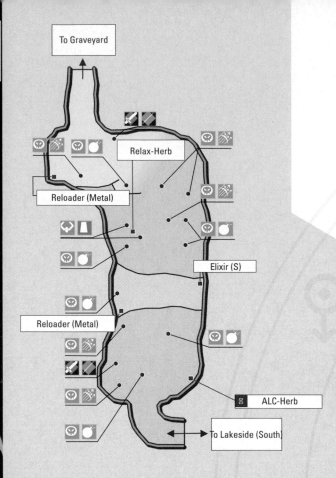

To Graveyard

Relax-Herb

Reloader (Metal)

Elixir (S)

Reloader (Metal)

ALC-Herb

To Lakeside (South)

GRAVEYARD

The redheaded girl places flowers on a gravesite then takes her leave, saying, "Bye, Sis." Al and Ed arrive and discuss the situation; they notice the white flower on the grave of none other than... Selene Eiselstein! The date of death on the tombstone is listed as just a few days after the boys left Heissgart. The pastor then appears and tells Ed the trains are out of service, and he invites the brothers into the safety of his church.

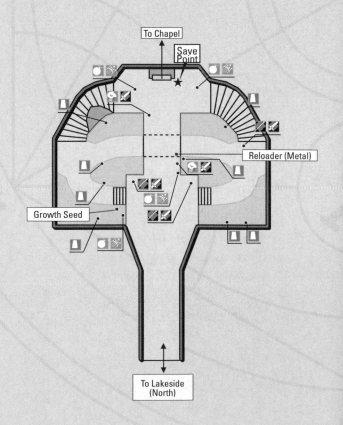

To Chapel

Save
Point

Reloader (Metal)

Growth Seed

To Lakeside
(North)

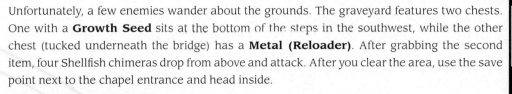

Unfortunately, a few enemies wander about the grounds. The graveyard features two chests. One with a **Growth Seed** sits at the bottom of the steps in the southwest, while the other chest (tucked underneath the bridge) has a **Metal (Reloader)**. After grabbing the second item, four Shellfish chimeras drop from above and attack. After you clear the area, use the save point next to the chapel entrance and head inside.

GAME BASICS

COMBAT TACTICS

CHARACTERS

EQUIPMENT

ENEMIES

WALKTHROUGH

STAGE 1: CENTRAL RAILROAD

STAGE 2: REMINESS GORGE

STAGE 3: HIESSGART

STAGE 4: NEW HIESSGART, PART 1

STAGE 5: NEW HIESSGART, PART 2

STAGE 6: NEW HIESSGART CASTLE

STAGE 7: HIESSGART ARMY FORTRESS

STAGE 8: UNDERGROUND WATERWAY

APPENDIX

CHAPEL

Inside, the pastor speaks of the "unholy beasts" that turned Hiessgart into a ghost town. He says the military remains curiously passive, letting the monsters run rampant. He also mentions that the best route to Central is via New Hiessgart, a settlement built by refugees from this town led by Professor Eiselstein. The boys agree to spend the night in the church, as sundown brings out more hordes of enemies. The pastor also tells them about Armony, the redheaded girl, and the mysterious death of Selene.

Meanwhile, outside, a pair of masked intruders approach. One is a tiger-like Masked Chimera—one we glimpsed earlier just before the Crab Chimera attack in the caves. The other, the big cat's master, is a woman. She sends the beast forward.

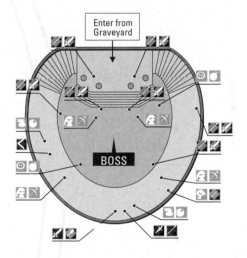

Enter from Graveyard

BOSS

As the pastor chats with the boys, the Masked Chimera suddenly bursts through the stained glass window of the sanctuary. It's boss time!

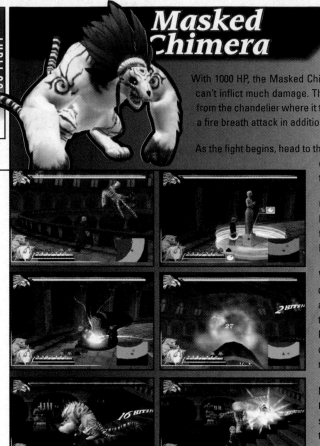

STAGE 3: HIESSGART

Central Plaza
Upper Suburbs
Central Plaza
Lower Suburbs
Wastelands
Lakeside (South)
Lakeside (North)
Graveyard
Chapel
Masked Chimera

S S FIGHT

Masked Chimera

HP	1000	HIT	40	SHOOT	36	ALC ATT	25	DEF	68
ALC DEF	100	EXP	500	ITEM OBTAINED	Training Manual				

With 1000 HP, the Masked Chimera can take a lot of punishment, and until you knock its mask off, you can't inflict much damage. This boss has a small arsenal of attacks. This boss starts the fight hanging from the chandelier where it tosses fireballs at both Ed and Al. Once the chimera is on the ground, it has a fire breath attack in addition to its normal attacks.

As the fight begins, head to the floor of the chapel and transmute the two benches into Crossbows—but do *not* get into them yet. Next, go up to the balcony and transmute one of the stone statues into a

Observe the Masked Chimera's attack pattern while climbing to the balcony. It tosses one or two fireballs at Ed, then turns its attention to Al, tossing another fireball or two. Dodge to avoid the fireballs, and when the boss's attention turns to Al, mount the Cannon and make every shot count.

When the boss gets knocked off the chandelier, dismount the Cannon and quickly leap down to the chapel floor. Call Al over to one of the Crossbows and have Ed jump into the other one. Wait for Al to hit the boss enough times so that its mask comes off, then start firing Ed's own Crossbow. Notice the difference in damage that occurs while the chimera's mask is off! You should be able to deplete about half of the boss's HP before it can recover its mask and jump back onto the chandelier.

Make use of the reloader items you've accumulated and reload both Crossbows. Then hustle back up to the balcony, transmute the other stone statue into a Cannon, and open fire to repeat the process. Keep it up until the Masked Chimera is defeated.

After the Masked Chimera falls, its master Camilla makes an appearance, and then exits. The pastor reappears and the boys discover a glowing feather that suddenly just... disappears. Strange!

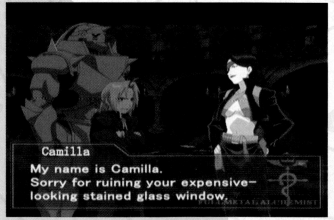

Camilla
My name is Camilla.
Sorry for ruining your expensive-looking stained glass window.

STAGE 4

NEW HIESSGART

Welcome to New Hiessgart, the refugee town. Things are quiet here—too quiet. Are alchemists really gathering en masse? There's only one way to find out. Hit the streets.

GAME BASICS

COMBAT TACTICS

CHARACTERS

EQUIPMENT

ENEMIES

WALKTHROUGH

STAGE 1:
CENTRAL
RAILROAD

STAGE 2:
REMINESS GORGE

STAGE 3:
HIESSGART

STAGE 4:
NEW HIESSGART,
PART 1

STAGE 5:
NEW HIESSGART,
PART 2

STAGE 6:
NEW HIESSGART
CASTLE

STAGE 7:
HIESSGART ARMY
FORTRESS

STAGE 8:
UNDERGROUND
WATERWAY

APPENDIX

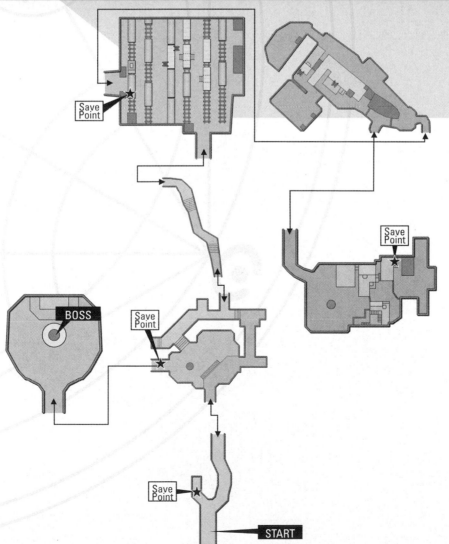

New Hiessgart
(Town Entry)
Central Plaza
Back Alley
Trainyard
Downtown
Drawbridge
Back to
Central Plaza
Station Plaza
The Alchemy
Brothers

NEW HIESSGART (TOWN ENTRY)

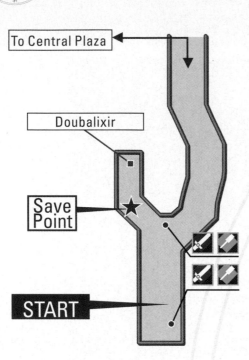

To Central Plaza

Doubalixir

Save Point

START

You start in a small alley that forks into two directions. The west fork leads to a save point, a chest with a **Doubalixir (S)**, and a dead end. The east fork leads to the town's central plaza.

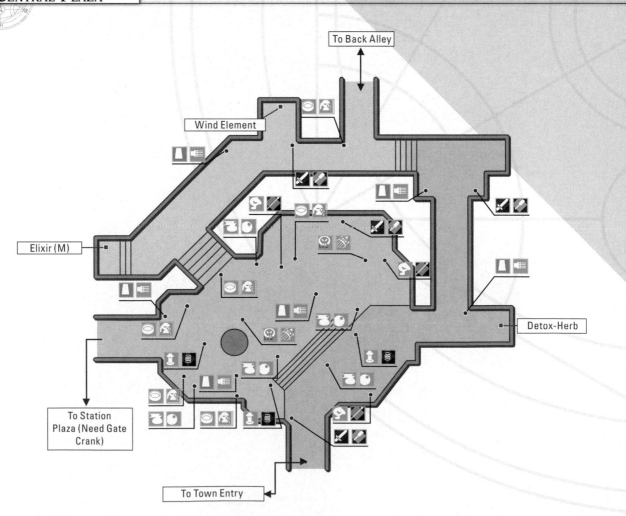

CENTRAL PLAZA

To Back Alley

Wind Element

Elixir (M)

Detox-Herb

To Station
Plaza (Need Gate
Crank)

To Town Entry

Alphonse wonders if the professor can provide information on some of the puzzling phenomena in Hiessgart, including the chimera infestation and the death of Selene. Then an Outlaw Alchemist runs into Ed, who drops his silver watch with the President's emblem and seal, the mark of a State Alchemist. Other outlaws object to a "dog of the military" being in town, and seek out one of their leaders, a highly inarticulate fellow named Blau.

Fight Blau and his Outlaw followers. Transmute the nearby Cannon to clear out other goons before focusing on Blau, but remember that he's the primary target. In fact, Blau is easier to defeat if you ignore the minions and concentrate all of your attacks on him.

After you hit Blau enough times, he runs off but calls in more Outlaws. This time your target is the Outlaw in the pink cloak. Most of the minions are just gunmen or swordsmen, but a few purple-hooded Outlaws have alchemy skills. Be ready to dodge their attacks, which heave up blocks of the street in a row toward Ed. Watch out for the pink-hooded outlaw's slick Gatling Gun attack, too.

After defeating the pink-hooded Outlaw, Ed appears at the gate to his intended destination, the Station Plaza. Unfortunately, the gate won't open without a special crank, which the Outlaw happens to carry. This provides a new objective: recover the gate crank from him. (He's now called Guy with Crank.)

Here you're free to wander around Central Plaza, which is crawling with Thugs and filled with sundry objects for your transmutation pleasure. Find a **Detox-Herb** by the southeast gate, a **Wind Element** up by the northwest gate, and an **Elixir (M)** by the gate to the west gate. Then exit via the north passage.

BACK ALLEY

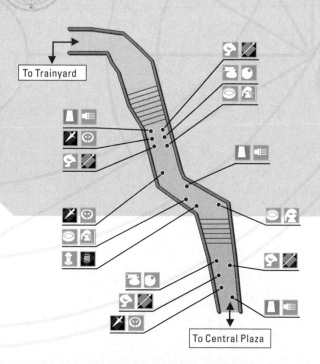

To Trainyard

To Central Plaza

A back alley is all about close quarters fighting, so its not a bad idea to transmute one of the fountains into a Gatling Gun and let Al mow down multiple enemies. Outlaws spawn both in front and behind you, so watch the map and don't let enemies sneak up unexpectedly. Transmute the umbrellas into Suction Machines and turn them on to gather up multiple enemies. Then wipe them out and continue north into the trainyard.

GAME BASICS
COMBAT TACTICS
CHARACTERS
EQUIPMENT
ENEMIES
WALKTHROUGH
STAGE 1: CENTRAL RAILROAD
STAGE 2: REMINESS GORGE
STAGE 3: HIESSGART
STAGE 4: NEW HIESSGART, PART 1
STAGE 5: NEW HIESSGART, PART 2
STAGE 6: NEW HIESSGART CASTLE
STAGE 7: HIESSGART ARMY FORTRESS
STAGE 8: UNDERGROUND WATERWAY
APPENDIX

STAGE 4:
NEW HIESSGART,
PART 1

New Hiessgart
(Town Entry)
Central Plaza
Back Alley
Trainyard
Downtown
Drawbridge
Back to
Central Plaza
Station Plaza
The Alchemy
Brothers

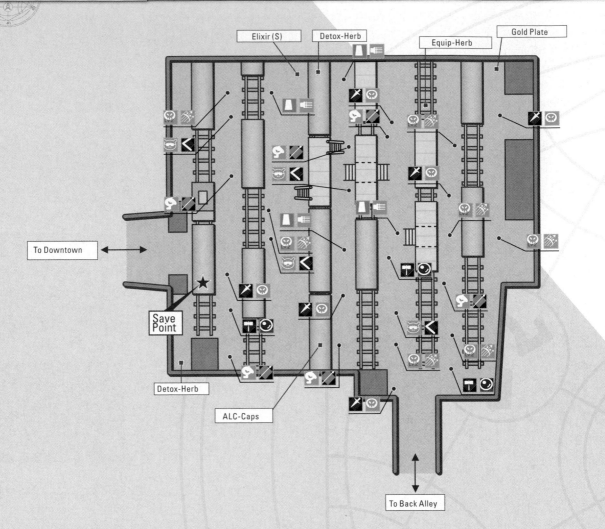

Elixir (S)

Detox-Herb

Equip-Herb

Gold Plate

To Downtown

Save Point

Detox-Herb

ALC-Caps

To Back Alley

Outlaws firing rifles from atop the train cars can be quite difficult. Transmute a Crossbow from one of the crates and take aim to get rid of them. Or better yet, first transmute the umbrella near the end of the cars into a Suction Machine to pull the trainhoppers to the ground.

Watch out for the beefed-up Gargoyle chimeras, too. This version spews poison as it flies overhead. If the pink cloud infects Ed (look for a trailing pink cloud), consume a Detox-Herb item to cure the ailment. When too many Gargoyles swarm around, call in Al for a Special Attack.

There's a **Gold Plate** inside a chest in the northeastern corner of the map; equip it on Al to gain its DEF +5 protection. Find an **Equip-Herb** behind the second row of train cars from the right (east).

PUT THE HAMMER DOWN

In the Trainyard, a new weapon helps you level up much more quickly. Transmute one of the wooden table sets into a Plastic Hammer. The Plastic Hammer inflicts damage of only 1 per hit on enemies no matter how strong you are, but it makes juggling and getting combos much easier—easier than any other weapon, in fact.

The fourth row of train cars extends the full length of the yard, so climb the ladder toward the north end of the row to get atop the train. There, nab the **Detox-Herb** (useful against poison-spewing Gargoyles) and **ALC-Caps** on either end of the cars.

Jump down to the west side of the train and head due north to find an **Elixir (S)** near the tunnel. Then go to the far southwest corner of the yard to find another **Detox-Herb**. The last train blocks the west exit to the downtown area, so approach the car with the yellow arrow. Press the ◉ button to pull the lever and move the train. Use the save point and head into the next section.

GAME BASICS

COMBAT TACTICS

CHARACTERS

EQUIPMENT

ENEMIES

WALKTHROUGH

STAGE 1:
CENTRAL
RAILROAD

STAGE 2:
REMINESS GORGE

STAGE 3:
HIESSGART

STAGE 4:
NEW HIESSGART,
PART 1

STAGE 5:
NEW HIESSGART,
PART 2

STAGE 6:
NEW HIESSGART
CASTLE

STAGE 7:
HIESSGART ARMY
FORTRESS

STAGE 8:
UNDERGROUND
WATERWAY

APPENDIX

DOWNTOWN

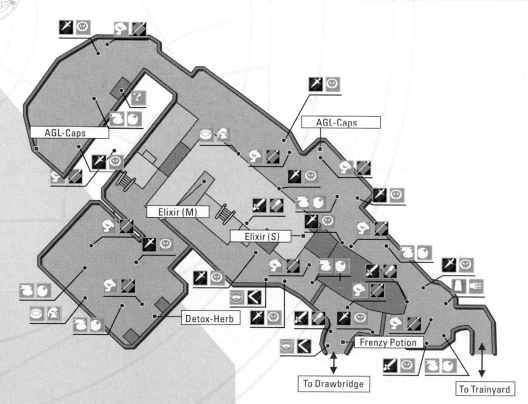

AGL-Caps

AGL-Caps

Elixir (M)

Elixir (S)

Detox-Herb

Frenzy Potion

To Drawbridge

To Trainyard

**STAGE 4:
NEW HIESSGART,
PART 1**

New Hiessgart
(Town Entry)

Central Plaza

Back Alley

Trainyard

Downtown

Drawbridge

Back to
Central Plaza

Station Plaza

The Alchemy
Brothers

Black-hatted Thugs and purple-hooded Outlaw alchemists attack immediately as you arrive. Pesky gunmen rain bullets down from the balconies in this area, too. Use the same strategy from the train yard; transmute umbrellas into Suction Machines that pull high shooters to the ground. The suction also keeps enemies grouped in a big cluster as long as the device is active. Quickly transmute a nearby Cannon and fire into the group to decimate their ranks.

Continue down the path to fight more Thugs and chimeras. Take advantage of the environmental objects or use some Special Attacks if you have any saved up. Don't miss the **AGL-Caps** in a corner as you walk northwest toward the bridge.

At the end of the bridge, you'll see the Guy with Crank (pink-hooded Outlaw) on a nearby rooftop and enemies appear in the open area. Quickly dispatch them all and don't miss the **AGL-Caps** hidden in the shadows. Then transmute the broken car into a stairway to access the rooftops.

Climb the stairs, turn right, and head southwest across the rooftop. Hop onto the low platform and place a Rockblocker to hop onto the next roof. This triggers a short dialogue: Ed thinks the culprit with the crank went over the fence on the roof to the southeast, but Al saw him running down below. (The fence gate is locked anyway, and you need a key.) Continue southwest and hop off the building at the ladder.

Go around the corner into an enclosed courtyard to meet Rot and his band of Outlaws and Thugs. This fight is similar to the one with Blau—focus on the main guy, not the minions, unless you want to rack up some EXP. After you defeat Rot, he leaves behind the **gate key** for the rooftop gate. Get the **Detox-Herb** by the southwest wall of the courtyard and return to the ladder on the side of the building where you jumped off.

Climb the ladder, turn right, and jump the gap over to the next building (the one with the fence). Find the gate and approach it, then watch Ed use the key to open the gate. Cross the roof to find a chest with an **Elixir (S)**, then jump off the building through the fence opening to the southwest. On the ground, turn left and find an **Elixir (M)** in a small alley on the northwest side of the building.

Head southeast toward the closed gate; wipe out any black-hat Thugs who appear. (Transmute and unleash a Poison Cow on the poor fools!) Open the gate using the control panel marked by a yellow arrow. Go through and clear out the Thugs from the street beyond. To the east is another closed gate that leads back to the area where you entered from the Trainyard, so don't open the second gate yet. Instead, exit via the south tunnel, picking up the **Frenzy Potion** in the process.

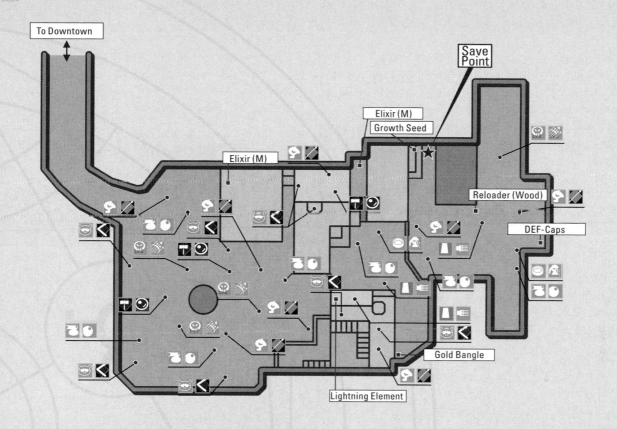

To Downtown

Save Point

Elixir (M)
Growth Seed

Elixir (M)

Reloader (Wood)

DEF-Caps

Gold Bangle

Lightning Element

GAME BASICS

COMBAT TACTICS

CHARACTERS

EQUIPMENT

ENEMIES

WALKTHROUGH

STAGE 1:
CENTRAL
RAILROAD

STAGE 2:
REMINESS GORGE

STAGE 3:
HIESSGART

STAGE 4:
NEW HIESSGART,
PART 1

STAGE 5:
NEW HIESSGART,
PART 2

STAGE 6:
NEW HIESSGART
CASTLE

STAGE 7:
HIESSGART ARMY
FORTRESS

STAGE 8:
UNDERGROUND
WATERWAY

APPENDIX

Climb the stairs to the large open plaza. Bad guys are plentiful, including some big-fisted, high-level Bouncers with hinged arms that fold into killer shotguns. Transmute everything in sight, putting Al into the large weapons and activating Suction Machines to bunch up enemy targets for him.

When the plaza is clear, proceed north up the small alley where large white tarps cover wooden crates, forming tiers like big steps. Jump onto the green roof of the building on the left and get the **Elixir (M)** in the chest. Jump back down and head southeast to climb up three sets of stairs to another rooftop.

Climb the roof shingles to a small platform, then place a Rockblocker and use it to jump onto the highest part of the roof. Find the chest with the **Lightning Element** next to a water tower. Jump off the east side of the building, nail the Thug and the Bouncer, and look for a chest in the corner containing a **Gold Bangle**. Now head to the gray boxes in the north and jump to the top of the building there.

On the roof, turn right and go down the slope; watch out for the rooftop gunmen to the east, though! Find a small hidden alley running north. A treasure chest containing an **Elixir (M)** sits at the alley's end. Hop back onto the roof, turn right, and climb the slope. Hop up past the barrels onto the flat roof and face east.

STAGE 4:
NEW HIESSGART,
PART 1

New Hiessgart
(Town Entry)
Central Plaza
Back Alley
Trainyard
Downtown
Drawbridge
Back to
Central Plaza
Station Plaza
The Alchemy
Brothers

DISK FOR DISTANCE

Transmute a barrel into a Boomerang, then transmute that into a Razor Ring. Toss the ring at the Thug snipers on the next roof to pick them off.

Jump east across the gap to the building with the three chimney stacks. The Thugs there should scatter. Continue forward and jump off from the *east* side of the building to get to the drawbridge. (Jumping off from any other side takes you back to the area between the plaza and the drawbridge and you'll have to make your way up to the roof again.) To the north you'll find a **Growth Seed** hidden behind the rectangular platforms.

While walking toward the drawbridge, look for a **Reloader (Wood)** item next to the building on the left and a **DEF-Caps** right in front of the drawbridge. The pink-hooded Outlaw awaits at the dead end to the east of the drawbridge. Defeat him to gain the crank.

A new save point appears next to the building with the three chimney stacks afterwards. After saving your game, head back over the rooftops to the downtown area and continue to Central Plaza (refer to the next map).

TAKE THE SHORTCUT

When you enter Downtown from the Drawbridge area, take an immediate right and open the gate. This lets you skip the entire downtown loop and head directly into the Trainyard.

BACK TO CENTRAL PLAZA

This map helps you retrace your route to Central Plaza. Along the way you must fight all of the same minions again, so stay on your toes. When you finally reach Central Plaza, use the crank at the Station Plaza entrance. Use the save point at the entrance to the Station Plaza, too. A big boss battle lies just ahead.

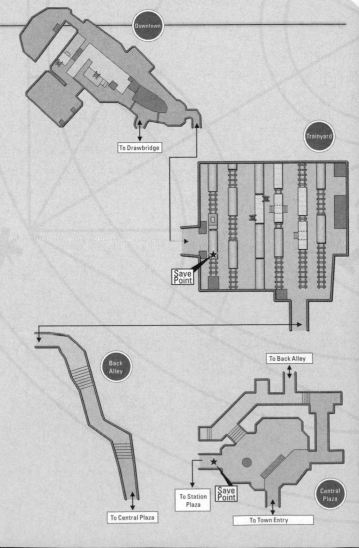

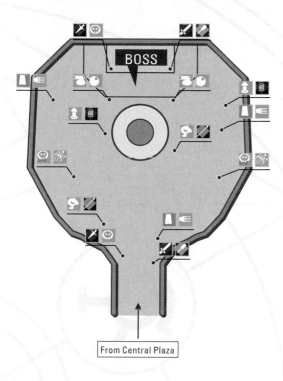

BOSS

From Central Plaza

Enter the plaza to see the redheaded girl, Armony, arguing vehemently with Rot, Gelb, and (sort of) Blau. She calls them "lying, no-good, alchemic poseurs" (Ooh, *zinger!*) for reneging on a promise to teach her alchemy.

Ed and Al step in just as Gelb tosses the girl across the square—fortunately, right into Ed's arms. Al gathers up Armony's scattered flowers, and Ed transmutes his Handblade, saying, "Now I've got a legitimate reason to kick some butt."

When the scene ends, the Outlaw alchemists attack Ed and Al. These purple-cloaked minions aren't particularly tough, so avoid using any of the transmutable objects in the plaza for this fight. Save the big stuff for the bigger fight that follows! After you defeat all of the minions, you must face four powerful bosses!

BOSS PREP WORK

You need big weapons for the upcoming boss fight. To save time later, transmute all nine of the big guns and suction-mouth devices in the plaza (but don't use them!) during the preliminary battle with the purple minions.

GAME BASICS

COMBAT TACTICS

CHARACTERS

EQUIPMENT

ENEMIES

WALKTHROUGH

STAGE 1: CENTRAL RAILROAD

STAGE 2: REMINESS GORGE

STAGE 3: HIESSGART

STAGE 4: NEW HIESSGART, PART 1

STAGE 5: NEW HEISSGART, PART 2

STAGE 6: NEW HIESSGART CASTLE

STAGE 7: HIESSGART ARMY FORTRESS

STAGE 8: UNDERGROUND WATERWAY

APPENDIX

New Hiessgart
(Town Entry)

Central Plaza

Back Alley

Trainyard

Downtown

Drawbridge

Back to
Central Plaza

Station Plaza

The Alchemy
Brothers

The Alchemy Brothers, Part 1

This boss fight can be *very* difficult if you don't have a good plan. Individually, the three brothers aren't that tough. The problem is multitasking: you must deal with all three at once *plus* avoid the living armor creature they create with their combined alchemy powers. Fortunately, with so many large transmutable weapons available in the plaza, you can avoid a lot of brutal hand-to-hand fighting.

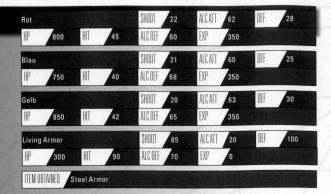

Rot		SHOOT	22	ALC ATT	62	DEF	28
HP	800	HIT	45	ALC DEF	60	EXP	350
Blau		SHOOT	21	ALC ATT	60	DEF	25
HP	750	HIT	40	ALC DEF	68	EXP	350
Gelb		SHOOT	20	ALC ATT	63	DEF	30
HP	850	HIT	42	ALC DEF	65	EXP	350
Living Armor		SHOOT	85	ALC ATT	20	DEF	100
HP	300	HIT	90	ALC DEF	70	EXP	0

ITEM OBTAINED Steel Armor

Immediately feed an AGL-Cap to both Ed and Al to speed up their run from weapon to weapon in the plaza and transmute all of the objects into large weapons: three Gatling Guns, two Crossbows, two Cannons, and two Suction Machines. The brothers and the Living Armor chase Ed relentlessly, so there's not much time to transmute an object, mount it, and fire it. Instead, transmute an object, move on, transmute another one, move on, and so forth until you transmute all nine objects.

Don't waste time and ammo on the Living Armor. When all three brothers go down, their alchemic creature collapses, so during the fight, just avoid the big metallic goon.

With all nine devices transmuted, immediately activate one of the suction-mouth devices to trap Rot, Gelb, and the suit of armor (Blau usually stays off in a corner by himself.)

Quickly put Al in the closest Gatling Gun and let him fire away. While Al is busy with the group, place Ed on a large weapon and join Al in the gunplay. When the ammo runs out, repeat the strategy with the other Suction Machine. With good aim, you can defeat one or even two of the brothers right off the bat.

When only Blau remains, use any remaining large weapons to finish him off. Watch out for his killer ice crystal attack, though.

Each of the brothers drops a valuable item upon his defeat, so don't go on a wild shooting spree and kill all three before you get a chance to pick up what they drop. Note that you can retrieve only two of the three items, since defeating the last brother takes you directly to a cut-scene.

Don't worry about it though, since you'll fight these brothers again. Just remember which brother you defeated last in this fight, and then defeat him first or second in the next round. For your reference: Rot drops the **Ripped Loincloth**, Gelb drops the **Lucky Bag**, and Blau drops the **Alchemy Guide**.

Ed and Al plan to head off to their destination, but Armony explains that no trains are running to Central for a couple of days, due to "some big derailment near Hiessgart." Then she demands to be taught the secrets of alchemy. She invites the boys to her house to meet her alchemist father.

NEW HIESSGART CASTLE

The Elric boys are surprised to discover that Armony's "home" is in fact a castle. But far more surprising is her father's identity. Professor Wilhelm Eiselstein is perhaps the most famous alchemist in the land, and the brothers know him from an earlier meeting. When Armony introduces the professor, he is cordial enough, but he forbids his daughter to learn alchemy.

When the girl leaves, Ed tries to bring up Selene but Wilhelm can't speak of her. But the wily fellow is quick to discern the Elric boys' attempt at human transmutation. He promises not to inform their master, Izumi. Finally, he introduces his assistants, Greta and Margot, and invites the boys to stay until the trains are running to Central again. Margot looks familiar to both Ed and Al, but she claims it's mistaken identity... a bit nervously.

In the end, the boys conclude the professor is hiding something. They decide to keep their ears open as they assist him in his research on catalytics, a process said to have much in common with the Philosopher's Stone. Meanwhile, Greta and Wilhelm discuss their "assistance" in the research, as well...

GAME BASICS

COMBAT TACTICS

CHARACTERS

EQUIPMENT

ENEMIES

WALKTHROUGH

STAGE 1:
CENTRAL
RAILROAD

STAGE 2:
REMINESS GORGE

STAGE 3:
HIESSGART

STAGE 4:
NEW HIESSGART,
PART 1

STAGE 5:
NEW HIESSGART,
PART 2

STAGE 6:
NEW HIESSGART
CASTLE

STAGE 7:
HIESSGART ARMY
FORTRESS

STAGE 8:
UNDERGROUND
WATERWAY

APPENDIX

STAGE 5:
NEW HEISSGART,
PART 2

Reminess Gorge
Revisited

New Hiessgart
Revisited

Hiessgart Revisited

New Hiessgart
Castle

Alchemyworks

Land Chimera

Genz Bresslau
(Version 2)

REMINESS GORGE REVISITED

To Mountain Pass (South)

Professor Eiselstein needs some etherflowers—"the best catalyst nature has to offer"—and mentions that some are growing back in Reminess Gorge. Time for some backtracking! The goal is to make it back to the Mountain Pass (South) area where you first encountered Armony. The group now grows to a threesome, as Armony joins Ed and Al!

ARMONY'S OKAY

Armony tags along on this errand. But as you encounter foes on the way, don't worry; the monsters cannot hurt her.

The enemies are the same as the first time through this area, so this portion of the walkthrough will just provide quick directions for travel. The trio starts near the lift in Cave (North). Head due south, jump off the ledge, and follow the curving passage to Cave (Center).

Continue south, then turn right at the bottom of the slope and head west down the corridor. This leads into Cave (South), but the trio will emerge right into a pack of Automail Panther and Gator-Boar chimeras!

Keep bearing south, descending the staircase that leads back out into Mountain Pass (North). Continue south through the narrow pass. Drop to the canyon floor and fight past some Gator-Boars and Winged Snakes to the ladder, then climb up to the platform. Continue south.

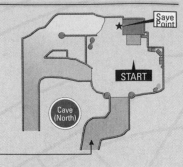

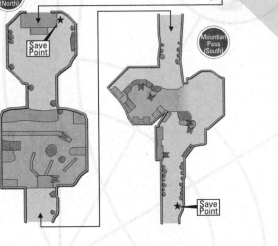

When you emerge into Mountain Pass (South), more chimeras attack. Fight them off and continue through the pass. After a brief cut-scene—no flowers anywhere!—save your game. After that, the group appears back in New Hiessgart.

To the Trainyard (Gelb)

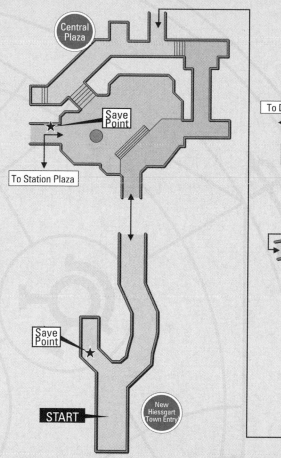

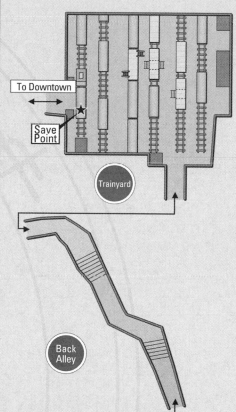

GAME BASICS

COMBAT TACTICS

CHARACTERS

EQUIPMENT

ENEMIES

WALKTHROUGH

STAGE 1:
CENTRAL
RAILROAD

STAGE 2:
REMINESS GORGE

STAGE 3
HIESSGA

STAGE 4:
NEW HIESSGART,
PART 1

STAGE 5:
NEW HIESSGART,
PART 2

STAGE 6:
NEW HIESSGART
CASTLE

STAGE 7:
HIESSGART ARMY
FORTRESS

STAGE 8:
UNDERGROUND
WATERWAY

APPENDIX

Back in the town entrance to New Hiessgart, the Alchemy Brothers flee from Ed and the others. The new objective is to find and interrogate each one of them. To find the first brother, Gelb, head north up the rightmost fork in the road to enter the Central Plaza. Hack through the various foes and head to the northern exit from the plaza.

Fight up the Back Alley to the Trainyard. Gelb's location is indicated by the blinking yellow dot on the map. He cowers on the rear platform of the single caboose on the east side of the yard. When you jump onto the platform, he states that his brother, Blau, might know where some etherflowers are located. He adds that Blau is in the Drawbridge area.

STAGE 5:
NEW HEISSGART,
PART 2

Reminess Gorge
Revisited

New Heissgart
Revisited

Hiessgart Revisited

New Heissgart
Castle

Alchemyworks

Land Chimera

Genz Bresslau
(Version 2)

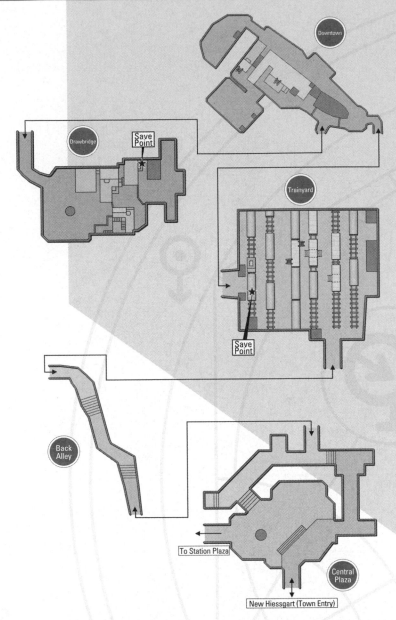

Exit the Trainyard to the west. As you enter the Downtown area, veer left and go east through the gate. Turn left into the tunnel to reach the Drawbridge area. Here, check the on-screen map for the yellow blinking dot that marks Blau's location. Next, continue southeast to the stairs leading up to the rooftops.

Face north and walk to the edge, then rotate the camera to change the view. There's Blau, hiding on a small ledge! Drop onto the ledge and approach him. Blau directs the trio (with the help of Armony's translation) to the Station Plaza to find the third brother, Rot.

Here's where it gets a little tricky. At the top of the stairs, climb the orange tile roof until you reach the flat white portion of the roof.

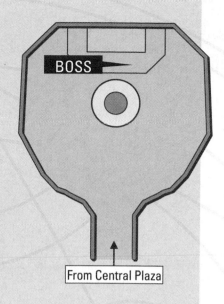

BOSS

From Central Plaza

Use the two previous maps to trace your way back through the southeast corner of Downtown, the Trainyard, and then down the Back Alley to Central Plaza. Before you head into the Station Plaza, save your game outside the station entrance.

Rot stands at the top of the steps across the plaza. Important: *Before* you speak to Rot, do what you did the last time you were in this plaza. Transmute *all* of the objects into large weapons (Crossbows, Cannons, Gatling Guns) and Suction Machines in preparation for the upcoming boss fight. Additional tip: Aim all guns at the suction-mouth devices first! After doing so, speak to Rot. His rotten brothers soon join him and decide it's payback time.

GAME BASICS

COMBAT TACTICS

CHARACTERS

EQUIPMENT

ENEMIES

WALKTHROUGH

STAGE 1:
CENTRAL RAILROAD

STAGE 2:
REMINESS GORGE

STAGE 3:
HIESSGART

STAGE 4:
NEW HIESSGART, PART 1

STAGE 5:
NEW HEISSGART, PART 2

STAGE 6:
NEW HEISSGART CASTLE

STAGE 7:
HIESSGART ARMY FORTRESS

STAGE 8:
UNDERGROUND WATERWAY

APPENDIX

BOSS FIGHT

The Alchemy Brothers, Part 2

This time around, the Alchemy Brothers summon not one but *five* living suits of armor to join in this little soiree. However, the strategy hasn't changed since the previous fight.

Rot				SHOOT	22	ALC ATT	62	DEF	28
HP	800	HIT	45	ALC DEF	60	EXP	350		
Blau				SHOOT	21	ALC ATT	60	DEF	25
HP	750	HIT	40	ALC DEF	68	EXP	350		
Gelb				SHOOT	20	ALC ATT	63	DEF	30
HP	850	HIT	42	ALC DEF	65	EXP	350		
Living Armors				SHOOT	85	ALC ATT	20	DEF	100
HP	300	HIT	90	ALC DEF	70	EXP	0		

ITEM OBTAINED	Alchemic Crystal

Activate one of the Suction Machines and *quickly* put Al in any large weapon closest to the group cluster. Then move Ed into a Gatling Gun or Crossbow and target Blau while the others remain incapacitated by the suction. This time, you want to defeat *first* the brother (most likely Blau) you defeated *last* in the previous battle to get the item he drops.

Remember, ignore the living armor warriors and concentrate on the three Alchemy Brothers. All five armor guys collapse when the last brother drops.

Repeat the tactic with the other Suction Machine, and focus all attacks on Blau. Once again, he'll run away, so mount the weapon closest to his current location or simply fight him hand to hand until he falls. After you pick up the item he drops, use the rest of the large weapons to defeat the remaining brothers.

The Alchemy Brothers reluctantly give up info about possible etherflower locations, sending you back to the "old town" of Hiessgart. Time for some more backtracking.

But first, watch the scene unfold back at Armony's castle. Professor Eiselstein speaks with Greta, his assistant, about a combat chimera developed for a local military commander. Then Greta asks Wilhelm about "the original wing." When they leave, the mystery deepens as Margot appears after eavesdropping.

STAGE 5:
NEW HEISSGART,
PART 2

Reminess Gorge
Revisited

New Hiessgart
Revisited

Hiessgart Revisited

New Hiessgart
Castle

Alchemyworks

Land Chimera

Genz Bresslau
(Version 2)

HIESSGART REVISITED

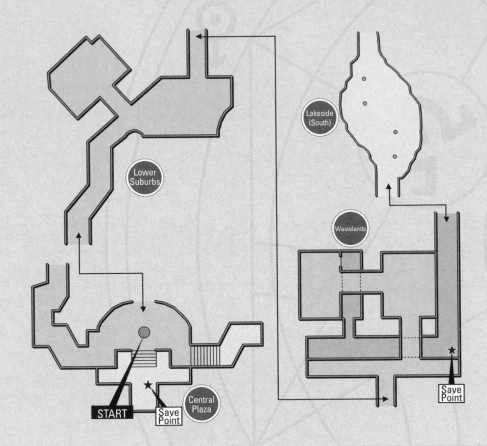

To Lakeside (South)

Back in Central Plaza in Hiessgart, the quest to find the etherflower continues. Armony suggests searching by the lake. Go through the Lower Suburbs into the Wastelands, and finally back to Lakeside (South). The etherflower is behind a pillar to the northwest. Unfortunately, just as Ed is about to pick the plant, a hungry Gator-Boar chimera makes a snack of it first

Now Ed must get Al to tackle the creature to force an unpleasant regurgitation. The quickest way is to hold down the R1 button and have Al guard Ed. This places Al directly in front of Ed. While still holding the R1 button, maneuver Ed and Al in front of the chimera as it approaches and quickly release and press the R1 button again to tackle the creature.

If you miss the first time, no problem: Just observe the creature's route as it circles the area in a repeating loop. Then stand Ed and Al directly in the creature's path, facing the direction the creature will approach, and hold the R1 button to guard Ed. When the creature gets close, press the R1 button again to trigger Al's tackle attack. Remember to face *directly toward* the running foe.

As luck would have it, this particular creature has an iron stomach. The beast rises and runs! After the cut-scene, you end up facing the archway at the south end of Lakeside (South). Run through the arch to automatically return to Central Plaza, bypassing the other areas in-between.

To Central Plaza

The Gator-Boar hides just around the corner to the southwest, behind a stone wall. Don't approach it from the front! Walk around and approach it from the side to avoid getting trampled when the beast charges out. Again, the Gator-Boar circles the fountain in a repeating loop.

As before, use Al's "Tackle" command to tackle the beast when it approaches. After the second successful tackle, the beast gets more aggressive, taking a bite out of Ed. After the fourth successful tackle, the chimera finally falls and (as Ed puts it) "horks up" the flower. Not a pretty sight.

Fortunately, Armony found some fresh etherflowers during the ruckus. All that work earns you a nice musical interlude as the boys bond with Armony and teach her the rudiments of alchemy.

STAND ASIDE
Position Ed *near* the Gator-Boar chimera's repeating path around the fountain, but not directly *in* the path. The beast will inflict serious damage if he runs over Ed.

GAME BASICS

COMBAT TACTICS

CHARACTERS

EQUIPMENT

ENEMIES

WALKTHROUGH

STAGE 1: CENTRAL RAILROAD

STAGE 2: REMINESS GORGE

STAGE 3: HIESSGART

STAGE 4: NEW HIESSGART, PART 1

STAGE 5: NEW HIESSGART, PART 2

STAGE 6: NEW HIESSGART CASTLE

STAGE 7: HIESSGART ARMY FORTRESS

STAGE 8: UNDERGROUND WATERWAY

APPENDIX

STAGE 5:
NEW HEISSGART,
PART 2

Reminess Gorge
Revisited

New Hiessgart
Revisited

Hiessgart Revisited

New Hiessgart
Castle

Alchemyworks

Land Chimera

Genz Bresslau
(Version 2)

Back in Armony's castle, Armony shows some unsettling signs of fatigue, dizziness, even illness. Suddenly, she collapses—and a single white wing appears on her back! As Alphonse says, "Like an angel!" Armony has trouble breathing and grows weaker.

The concerned boys decide to take Armony to her father. On the way they encounter chimeras in the castle's central courtyard! Is the professor in trouble? Then Armony directs them away from the castle to a basement laboratory in the Alchemyworks.

Alphonse
A wing... A wing, Ed. A wing!
Armony's got a wing on her back...
Like an angel!

Armony
No, not the castle, Ed...
Over there... He's in his lab...
He's in the Alchemyworks...

Central Courtyard

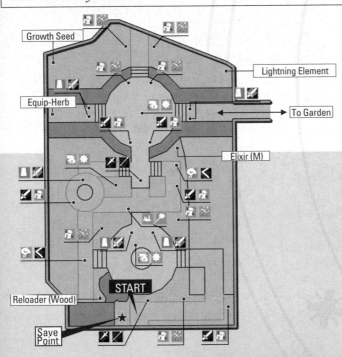

Growth Seed

Lightning Element

Equip-Herb

To Garden

Elixir (M)

Reloader (Wood)

START

Save Point

Note the save point directly west of where you start. Fight past the chimeras along the paved path; transmute the small tree into a Crossbow and put Al in it. Follow the path up onto the raised circular platform, then go down the west stairs and find the **Reloader (Wood)** item against the building.

Transmute the nearby Suction Machine and, further north (toward the fountain), another Crossbow. Put Al in the Crossbow and activate the suction to pull the Gargoyles out of the sky into a ball of juicy Crossbow targets.

Proceed east through the broken gap in the raised walkway. Follow the stone path north and look for the chest containing an **Elixir (M).** Take the steps leading back up to the next circular platform in the north to find steps to three gates (plus another contingent of chimera attackers). Clear the platform of enemies before turning your attention to the gates.

First, approach the west gate. A giant Military Crab drops when you get close to the chest. Go back up the steps and transmute the tree on the platform into a Crossbow, and shoot the arrows *over* the crustacean (they track targets) to hit him. (Alternate tactic: Transmute the two sculptures on the path into Monoliths and knock them over on top of the crab.) When the creature dies, claim the **Equip-Herb** inside the chest.

Now go north down the steps to a gate with a large grassy area on either side of it. The chest in the grassy area to the west contains a **Growth Seed**. Pick it up, then transmute the two small trees into Crossbows and put Al in the easternmost one.

Go east toward another chest that contains a **Lightning Element**. Another Military Crab drops to defend this latter item, but Al should gun him down quickly with the Crossbow. Go back upstairs and try to exit the area via the eastern gate. Yet another Military Crab drops. Shoot this beast with Crossbows or knock a Monolith onto it, then proceed through the gate.

GAME BASICS

COMBAT TACTICS

CHARACTERS

EQUIPMENT

ENEMIES

WALKTHROUGH

STAGE 1: CENTRAL RAILROAD

STAGE 2: REMINESS GORGE

STAGE 3: HIESSGART

STAGE 4: NEW HIESSGART, PART 1

STAGE 5: NEW HIESSGART, PART 2

STAGE 6: NEW HIESSGART CASTLE

STAGE 7: HIESSGART ARMY FORTRESS

STAGE 8: UNDERGROUND WATERWAY

APPENDIX

Garden

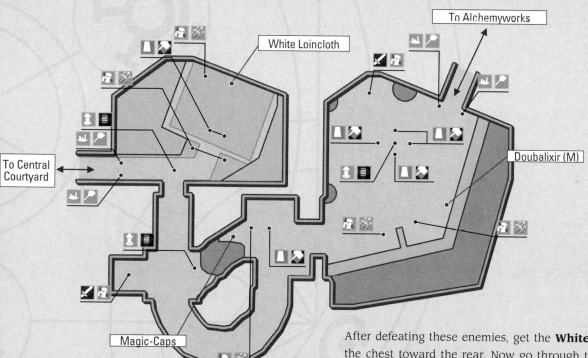

To Alchemyworks

White Loincloth

Doubalixir (M)

To Central Courtyard

Magic-Caps

The Gargoyles in this area are plentiful and deadly with their new fireball attacks, so blast them as fast as possible. Hustle up the steps from where you entered and transmute the two trees into Crossbows. Have Al man one while Ed takes the other. This should provide enough ammo to drop all the flying chimeras, as well as the giant Military Crab guarding the grassy area.

After defeating these enemies, get the **White Loincloth** in the chest toward the rear. Now go through the arches and venture into the atrium. Around the U-shaped bend, nail the Military Crab to get the **Magic-Caps** item in the chest behind the tree. (For an easier method, transmute the tree into a Crossbow and put Al to work.)

At the next courtyard, annihilate all of the enemies there and get the **Doubalixir (M)** item in the eastern corner. Upon doing so, move on toward the huge Alchemyworks structure.

STAGE 5:
NEW HEISSGART,
PART 2

Reminess Gorge
Revisited

New Hiessgart
Revisited

Hiessgart Revisited

New Hiessgart
Castle

Alchemyworks

Land Chimera

Genz Bresslau
(Version 2)

ALCHEMYWORKS

Entry

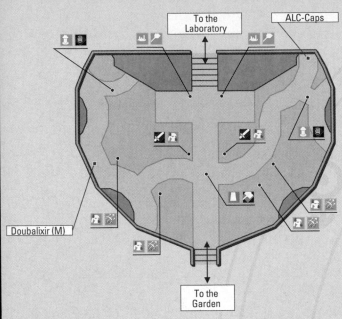

Watch out for the high-level Gator-Boar with its new alchemy attack that uproots rows of the ground. Don't miss the **ALC-Caps** in one corner and a **Doubalixir (M)** hugging the wall on the opposite end. Go up the steps and through the doors when you're done.

Entry

Use the save point immediately to the west of the lab entrance. The waterfalls on the room's east side run off into a moat, where a chest containing the **Combo Guide** sits underneath the second set of waterfalls. Look for a **Growth Seed** underneath one of the tables, too. Then climb the nearby ladder up to the support beams.

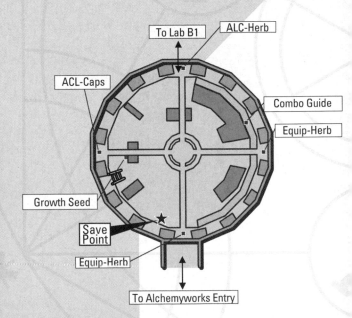

Treasure chests sit on each end of the support beams. To get the closest one, jump toward the support beam and in midair change Ed's direction so that he lands next to the chest. This one

contains an **ALC-Caps**, and from there, walk across the beams to get the other three chests containing an **ALC-Herb** and two **Equip-Herbs**. Drop back to the floor and head north into the basement.

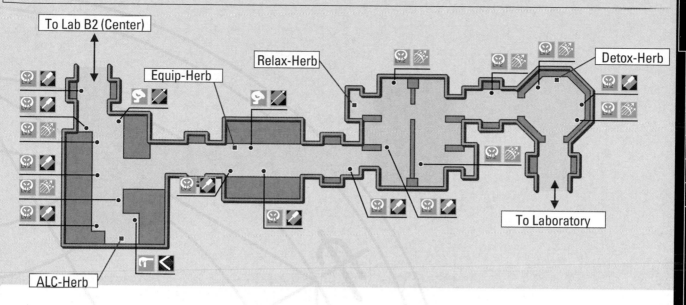

To Lab B2 (Center)

Equip-Herb

Relax-Herb

Detox-Herb

ALC-Herb

To Laboratory

GAME BASICS

COMBAT TACTICS

CHARACTERS

EQUIPMENT

ENEMIES

WALKTHROUGH

STAGE 1:
CENTRAL
RAILROAD

STAGE 2:
REMINESS GORGE

STAGE 3:
HIESSGART

STAGE 4:
NEW HIESSGART,
PART 1

STAGE 5:
NEW HIESSGART,
PART 2

STAGE 6:
NEW HIESSGART
CASTLE

STAGE 7:
HIESSGART ARMY
FORTRESS

STAGE 8:
UNDERGROUND
WATERWAY

APPENDIX

Some Winged Snakes and Electro-Slugs guard a chest containing a **Detox-Herb** on the octagon-shaped platform. Exterminate the pests, loot the chest, and continue down the path until you reach a room divided by a chain fence... and crawling with slugs.

Look for a **Relax-Herb** on one of the platforms and keep moving along the path. This triggers a cut-scene: the boys move cautiously down a path with large glass incubators on either side. Chimeras! Is there a link between Armony's wing and the glowing feather you found back at the church?

SPECIAL SWARM
Counter swarms of many enemies (such as Electro-Slugs and/or Winged Snakes) with a Special Attack or two.

Suddenly, a pair of blue Gorilla-Goat attacks up the aisle. These monsters can use alchemy to create big synthetic cannons. After you defeat them, continue west. Find the **Equip-Herb** chest along the way, and nab an **ALC-Herb** on the southwest end of the T-intersection at the end of the path. Then head north.

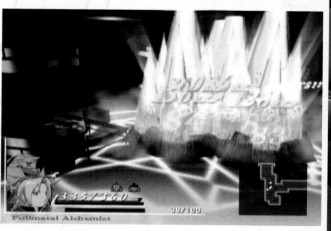

STAGE 5:
NEW HEISSGART,
PART 2

Reminess Gorge
Revisited

New Hiessgart
Revisited

Hiessgart Revisited

New Hiessgart
Castle

Alchemyworks

Land Chimera

Genz Bresslau
(Version 2)

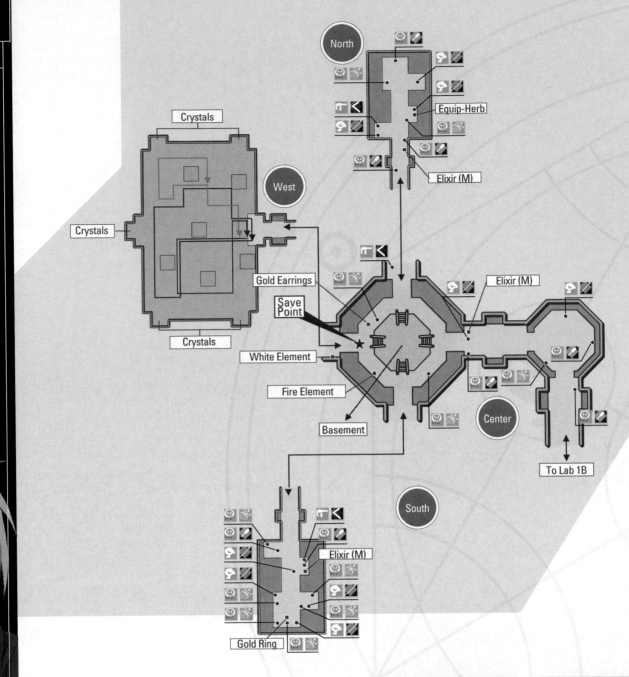

As you can see on the map, Lab B2 is a sprawling, multi-compartment complex with rooms branching to the north, south, and west. You arrive in the anteroom of the lab's central hub.

Lab B2 (Center)

Clear the octagonal anteroom of enemies and proceed west along the corridor toward a bigger room with a huge octagonal pit; stop to find the **Elixir (M)** (right side) along the way. Al points out the four "funky" designs on the walkway around the edge of the pit. Ed thinks they resemble transmutation circles, but like none he's ever seen before.

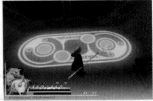

Walk around the pit and open the chest to acquire a **Fire Element**. Jump down into the pit, use the save point, and open the chest with the **Gold Earrings** near the wall. Climb one of the ladders back to the upper level. Use the exit at the south end of the room first.

Lab B2 (South)

Transmute objects into large weapons and Suction Machines while moving down the corridor. Don't miss the chest containing an **Elixir (M)** as you walk down the corridor toward the crystal at the end of the room. A **Gold Ring** is hidden right behind the crystal. Put Al in one of the large weapons near the crystal so he can go on the offensive immediately when monsters appear.

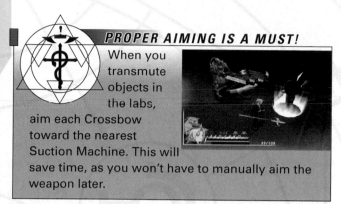

PROPER AIMING IS A MUST!

When you transmute objects in the labs, aim each Crossbow toward the nearest Suction Machine. This will save time, as you won't have to manually aim the weapon later.

Now it's time to destroy the crystal. Stand on the side closest to the Suction Machine, then take a whack at the crystal; one hit with any weapon should do the trick. Be ready, though! Once the crystal shatters, angry monsters swarm the room, including a gruesome and poisonous creeping hodgepodge, a creature that resembles a genetics experiment gone horribly awry. Immediately trigger the nearby Suction Machine to freeze the beasts in place, then hop into a large weapon and help Al clean house.

Stay wary as you return north toward the central hub, as additional creatures make an appearance in hopes of cutting off the exit. In the center room, veer left and go to the west exit.

Lab B2 (West)

Don't miss the **Wind Element** right outside the entrance to Lab B2 (West). Inside, the objective is to destroy all five crystals in the wall alcoves using a Cannon mounted on a moving platform. The platform can move around the room on one of three colored tracks. You can switch track layouts (yellow, blue, or green), cycling through them by pulling the lever marked by the yellow arrow. Check the map for the exact paths.

Huge pumping machinery blocks your shot from certain angles in the room. The best track layout is blue. The blue path takes you completely around the room, whereas the yellow and green paths favor either side of the room respectively. Once you step on the platform, it automatically moves along the path around the room, so quickly mount the Cannon and shoot the crystals as they come into view. When all five crystals are destroyed, return to the central hub and go to the north exit.

Lab B2 (North)

Use the same strategy here as you used for Lab B2 (South). Transmute objects into large weapons while walking down the corridor, picking up the **Elixir (M)** and **Equip-Herb** along the way. Put Al into the Quintuple Crossbow closest to the crystal at the end of the room, then destroy the crystal. Wipe out the waves of chimeras that attack, then return to the central hub.

Lab B2 (Center)

After you've visited all three rooms from the central hub of Lab B2 and destroyed all seven crystals, the alchemy circles in front of each entrance should be glowing yellow. Hop into the yellow circle at the bottom of the hole and an elevator activates, dropping Ed and Al to a lower level. There, walk up the corridor until you meet the injured Professor Eiselstein. He admits creating the chimeras, but claims he did it for Armony. Suddenly, the ground shakes.

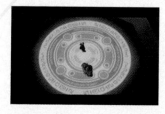 

GAME BASICS

COMBAT TACTICS

CHARACTERS

EQUIPMENT

ENEMIES

WALKTHROUGH

STAGE 1: CENTRAL RAILROAD

STAGE 2: REMINESS GORGE

STAGE 3: HIESSGART

STAGE 4: NEW HIESSGART, PART 1

STAGE 5: NEW HEISSGART, PART 2

STAGE 6: NEW HEISSGART CASTLE

STAGE 7: HIESSGART ARMY FORTRESS

STAGE 8: UNDERGROUND WATERWAY

APPENDIX

STAGE 5:
NEW HEISSGART,
PART 2

Reminess Gorge
Revisited

New Hiessgart
Revisited

Hiessgart Revisited

New Hiessgart
Castle

Alchemyworks

Land Chimera

Genz Bresslau
(Version 2)

Laboratory

You automatically return to the Laboratory after you speak to the professor. It's a *very* good idea to save your game at this point, as you're about to engage in two consecutive boss fights. Before you save and go outside, however, read the "Get a Firebomb" tip. Exit the lab via the south door and continue south across the Alchemyworks entry yard.

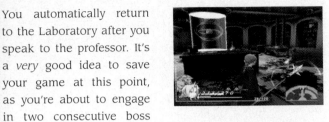

GET A FIREBOMB

Before you go outside to the garden, return to Lab B1. Run the length of the corridor to the T-intersection. There, transmute the steel drum into a Flamethrower. This will come in handy in the fight against the land chimera.

Alchemyworks Garden

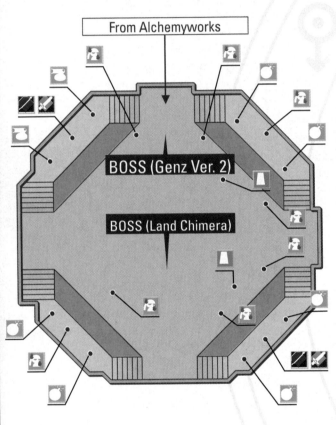

From Alchemyworks

BOSS (Genz Ver. 2)

BOSS (Land Chimera)

When you reach the garden, a gargantuan combat chimera smashes through the wall and enters. Led by soldiers and a high-rank military officer named Nemda, the beast is a drooling monstrosity. Within moments, it goes berserk and out of control! And soon it threatens to attack Armony...

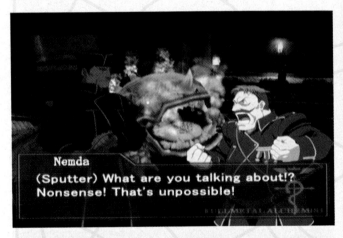

Nemda
(Sputter) What are you talking about!? Nonsense! That's unpossible!

Land Chimera

HP	1000	HIT	80	SHOOT	80	ALC ATT	50	DEF	80
ALC DEF	180	EXP	2000	ITEM OBTAINED	Armlet of Penetration				

The Land Chimera may look intimidating, but once you understand its weakness it's not too difficult to defeat. Regular attacks barely hurt this boss, so hand-to-hand fighting is not the answer. The way to conquer this beast is from the inside out.

The Land Chimera has three methods of attack. Its main attack is a slew of tracking fireballs that are tough to dodge. Occasionally, the boss stomps the floor, sending out a wave of energy. Finally, the creature tries to suck its foes into its mouth, causing *immense* damage.

The best strategy is to pop an AGL-Cap item for added speed, then run around the garden avoiding the boss's first two attacks while paying close attention to the spouts on its back. Before the boss tries its suction attack, it always ejects a load of explosive shells from these back spouts. Transmute the shells into Bombs and push them into the path of the suction the beast creates so they'll explode inside the creature.

Don't ignite the Bombs first! They go off just fine once they are swallowed. Four bombs will do the trick. If you acquired a Flamethrower, you're already holding a bomb before the fight even begins. When you see the land chimera eject its first shells, drop the Flamethrower in front of the creature and transmute it into a Bomb. This way you don't have to chase down shells and push around transmuted Bombs.

If you're fast enough, you can try to get more than one Bomb into the boss's mouth each time it tries to suck you in, and the damage will stack. As a matter of fact, it's the best way to get the S-Rank!

Brigadier General Nemda is despondent about the loss of his beloved combat chimera. In fact, he's so upset that he orders the arrest of Ed and Al. Then Genz reappears, sheathed in even more automail than before and itching for revenge.

Genz
Heh heh heh...
Looks like it's finally my turn...

GAME BASICS

COMBAT TACTICS

CHARACTERS

EQUIPMENT

ENEMIES

WALKTHROUGH

STAGE 1: CENTRAL RAILROAD

STAGE 2: REMINESS GORGE

STAGE 3: HIESSGART

STAGE 4: NEW HIESSGART, PART 1

STAGE 5: NEW HIESSGART, PART 2

STAGE 6: NEW HIESSGART CASTLE

STAGE 7: HIESSGART ARMY FORTRESS

STAGE 8: UNDERGROUND WATERWAY

APPENDIX

BOSS FIGHT

STAGE 5:
NEW HEISSGART,
PART 2

Reminess Gorge
Revisited

New Hiessgart
Revisited

Hiessgart Revisited

New Hiessgart
Castle

Alchemyworks

Land Chimera

Genz Bres
(Version 2)

Genz Bresslau
(Version 2)

HP	1250	HIT	83	SHOOT	65	ALC ATT	55	DEF	45
ALC DEF	130	EXP	1500	ITEM OBTAINED	Bulletproof Vest				

Genz brings back all of his attacks from the first battle, plus he adds a drop-kick combo to his punch. He also has a killer spray attack, unleashing a wave of bullets from his arms. Finally, he blocks a lot more this time around.

Fortunately, the arena is much bigger than before, so avoiding his attacks is much easier, especially if you consume an AGL-Cap. To defeat Genz, transmute both of the lampposts on the raised balcony into Cannons and simply unload on him. When the first Cannon runs out, run over to the other one. Shoot and repeat, again and again.

If you reload the Cannons fast enough, Genz won't be able to get onto the platform where Ed will be shooting. If you have a Frenzy Special Attack saved up, use that to knock off a huge chunk of his HP as well.

Theoretically, you can repeat the cannon attacks until Genz falls, but if you run out of Reloader (Metal) items you'll have to fight him up close and personal. If this occurs, don't expect to trap him in a corner and just "button mash." Even if you manage to knock him down, he'll throw his wicked elbows if you're anywhere close to him when he gets up.

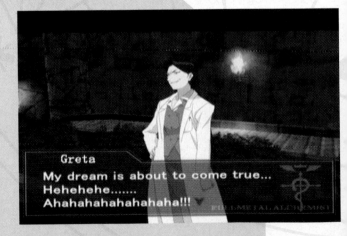

Transmute a Dagger (there's one in the area) and put a Wind Element on it. Lure Genz close and get him to do his charging punch attack. Avoid it by sidestepping, then slip around behind him to get in a combo with the Wind Dagger.

When the fight ends, Genz escapes but Brigadier Nemda insists on arresting Ed and Al. He surrounds the boys with his soldiers. When Colonel Roy Mustang and Major Armstrong suddenly appear, Ed thinks he's saved, but the Colonel allows Nemda to take both brothers into custody... and to prepare them for a court martial!

Meanwhile, Armony continues to deteriorate. And the mystery of Greta, the professor's assistant, continues to grow.

Greta
My dream is about to come true...
Hehehehe.......
Ahahahahahahahaha!!!

STAGE 6
HIESSGART FORTRESS

This stage begins with a short cut-scene: Colonel Mustang and Major Armstrong offer a ride to a water-splashed "pedestrian" and get the inside scoop on what's going on at New Hiessgart Castle. Lieutenant Hawkeye confirms some suspected links, revealing the true nature of the chimera incidents. It seems Brigadier Nemda is fostering plans for a private army. And the professor's assistant, Greta, is planted firmly beneath Mustang's umbrella of suspicion.

Meanwhile, down in the holding cells of the Hiessgart army fortress, a couple of frisky "decoys" are hatching a plan of escape…

GAME BASICS

COMBAT TACTICS

CHARACTERS

EQUIPMENT

ENEMIES

WALKTHROUGH

STAGE 1:
CENTRAL
RAILROAD

STAGE 2:
REMINESS GORGE

STAGE 3:
HIESSGART

STAGE 4:
NEW HIESSGART,
PART 1

STAGE 5:
NEW HIESSGART,
PART 2

STAGE 6:
NEW HIESSGART
CASTLE

STAGE 7:
HIESSGART ARMY
FORTRESS

STAGE 8:
UNDERGROUND
WATERWAY

APPENDIX

Hiessgart Fortress

STAGE 6:
NEW HIESSGART
CASTLE

Holding Cells

Fortress Compound
(South)

Fortress Compound
(North)

Fortress 1F

Fortress 2F (West)

Fortress 2F (East)

Fortress 3F (East)

Fortress 3F (West)

Fortress 3F (East)

Fortress 4F (East)

Fortress 4F (West)

Fortress 4F (East)

Fortress Rooftop

Sky Chimera

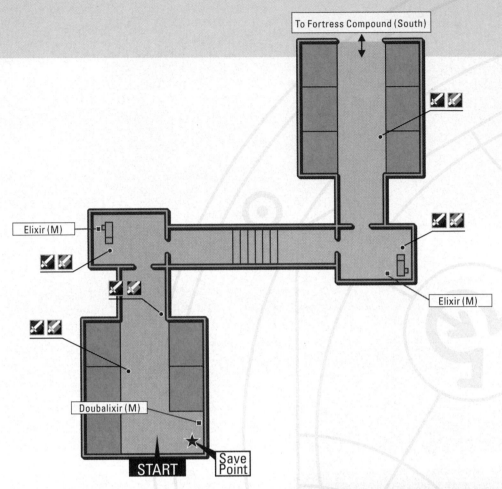

To Fortress Compound (South)

Elixir (M)

Elixir (M)

Doubalixir (M)

START

Save
Point

Open the treasure chest on the bunk to find a **Doubalixir (M)**. Walk down the hall and transmute a Sword for Ed and add a Fire Element if you want. Continue down the hall and defeat the team of Junior State MPs. (They're not too tough, especially if you transmute the chair into a Sword for Al.) Nab the **Elixir (M)** behind the desk. Continue east down the hall and up the stairs to another guard room. Defeat the MP guards and get another **Elixir (M)** near the desk. Fight north to the end of the next hall to exit.

Soldier B
Escape in progress!
Capture them!!!

FULLMETAL ALCHEMIST

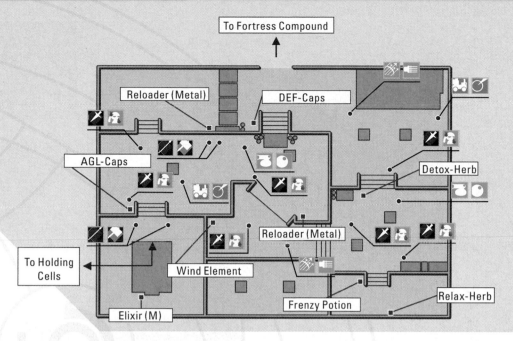

To Fortress Compound

Reloader (Metal)

DEF-Caps

AGL-Caps

Detox-Herb

Reloader (Metal)

To Holding Cells

Wind Element

Relax-Herb

Elixir (M)

Frenzy Potion

GAME BASICS

COMBAT TACTICS

CHARACTERS

EQUIPMENT

ENEMIES

WALKTHROUGH

STAGE 1: CENTRAL RAILROAD

STAGE 2: REMINESS GORGE

STAGE 3: HIESSGART

STAGE 4: NEW HIESSGART, PART 1

STAGE 5: NEW HIESSGART, PART 2

STAGE 6: NEW HIESSGART CASTLE

STAGE 7: HIESSGART ARMY FORTRESS

STAGE 8: UNDERGROUND WATERWAY

APPENDIX

View the interesting dialogue between Brigadier Nemda and, *gasp*, Greta, who reveals a somewhat nefarious plan. Nemda calls for the arrest of both the professor and his daughter. Sounds like Armony's in trouble... or will be, soon.

AVOID THE LIMELIGHT

The guard towers in the compound feature not only searchlights but painful machine guns. Stay out of their beams of light!

When you regain control of Ed, whack the pair of sword-wielding MPs and locate the **Elixir (M)** behind the building. Go up the steps to the north and make a sharp left-hand turn to pick up the **AGL-Caps** around the corner.

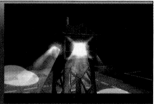

VESTED INTEREST

Equip Ed with the Bulletproof Vest accessory as he crosses the fortress yard. The vest reduces gun damage by 25 percent, so Ed suffers less if he gets caught in the guard tower spotlights.

Continue north, dodging searchlights as you hustle to the steps leading down to a storage yard. Knock out the MP guards and grab the **Reloader (Metal)** item near the covered boxes. Climb back up the stairs and sneak east past both guard towers, cutting across the middle of the yard toward

the ramp leading down. Find the **Reloader (Metal)** chest just left of the ramp, then descend the ramp to view a cutscene—Ed and Al discern the way out, but there's too much security blocking the way.

Grab the **Wind Element** in the far corner and head east. Transmute a Gatling Gun near the eastern ramp and have Al man it; he'll pick off the guard up the ramp. There, two guard towers overlook the southeastern part of the compound. Climb the ramp and turn right, hugging the perimeter as you head toward the south staircase. Go down the stairs and neutralize the two MPs, then loot the two chests in the area for a **Relax-Herb** and a **Frenzy Potion**.

Go back upstairs and head north across the yard, avoiding the lights. Get the **Detox-Herb** from the chest near the far steps, then walk down. Head north toward the H2 Building, then proceed west toward the archway exit. Before leaving the area, look on the west side of the steps that are blocked by the large covered boxes. A **DEF-Caps** item is hidden just around the corner.

STAGE 6: NEW HIESSGART CASTLE

Holding Cells

Fortress Compound (South)

Fortress Compound (North)

Fortress 1F

Fortress 2F (West)

Fortress 2F (East)

Fortress 3F (East)

Fortress 3F (West)

Fortress 3F (East)

Fortress 4F (East)

Fortress 4F (West)

Fortress 4F (East)

Fortress Rooftop

Sky Chimera

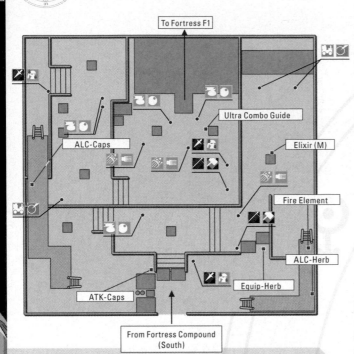

The next goal is to reach the tall building to the north, which is the fortress headquarters. Go east toward the ladder. Before venturing to the catwalks above, however, pick up the **Equip-Herb** next to the covered boxes and the **ALC-Herb** underneath the catwalk in the southeast corner of the map. After doing so, go ahead and climb the ladder.

Follow the catwalk to the end, jump down, and grab the **Fire Element** underneath the catwalk. Run past the Two-Headed Dog and the guard tower and transmute the boxes into two slick new vehicles, a Tank and a Steamroller. Put Al in the Tank and make Ed hop into the Steamroller as a squad of MPs attacks! Nail them all, then hop out and get the **Elixir (M)** near the guard tower. Remember to avoid those searchlights!

Go south, hugging the wall on the right side, and turn right. Transmute what appears to be a machine gun into a bigger, more powerful Gatling Gun and let Al man it. He'll pump a lot of rounds into the

Two-Headed Dog pacing at the top of the ramp ahead. Reload the Gatling Gun so Al can finish the job, then run up the ramp to lure the MPs back toward Al.

Proceed west past the guard tower and go down the stairs on the opposite side of the platform, then battle the MP and dogs. Look for the **ATK-Caps** item near the covered boxes. Climb the ladder to the next catwalk. Run through the spotlight that suddenly turns on when you're up there. At the end of the catwalk, drop down to the next area.

Ascend the next set of steps and turn right, fighting south past the pair of Two-Headed Dogs. (Transmute the nearby Cannons for extra firepower.) When you get past the second guard tower, find the **ALC-Caps** next to the west wall underneath the catwalk.

Head due east down the steps to trigger a cut-scene. Soon more MPs and guard dogs flood the yard! You must defeat all of them to move onward. Transmute the Gatling Guns for Al and watch his back as he swings the big gun around. After the fight, find the **Ultra Combo Guide** next to one of the guard towers. Then go inside the Fortress headquarters building.

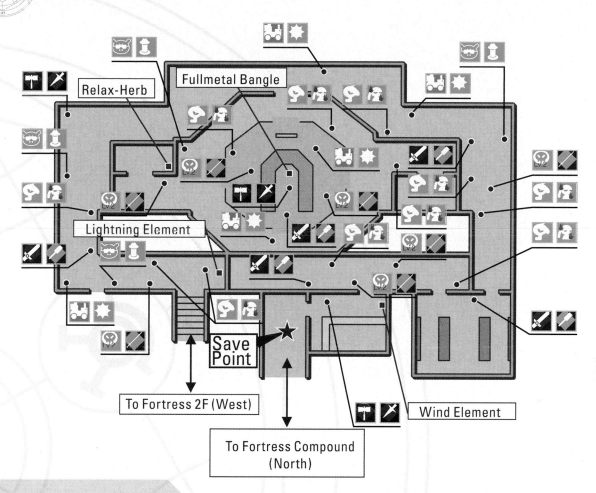

Relax-Herb

Fullmetal Bangle

Lightning Element

Save Point

To Fortress 2F (West)

To Fortress Compound (North)

Wind Element

GAME BASICS

COMBAT TACTICS

CHARACTERS

EQUIPMENT

ENEMIES

WALKTHROUGH

STAGE 1:
CENTRAL
RAILROAD

STAGE 2:
REMINESS GORGE

STAGE 3:
HIESSGART

STAGE 4:
NEW HIESSGART,
PART 1

STAGE 5:
NEW HIESSGART,
PART 2

STAGE 6:
NEW HIESSGART
CASTLE

STAGE 7:
HIESSGART ARMY
FORTRESS

STAGE 8:
UNDERGROUND
WATERWAY

APPENDIX

Save your game and take the door to the east to search the next room for a **Wind Element**. Several Two-Headed Dogs patrol the hallway beyond; rush into the hall, turn left, and transmute the Suction Machine to pull all of the dogs together. Annihilate the canine freaks, head east, and take the first right into the locker room.

Nothing here! Head out the other door and follow the hallway to a confrontation with a squad of intermediate-level MPs. After the fight, continue past a large briefing room with glass walls and flags hanging inside. Defeat the trio of MP Chiefs who attack and move on. Follow the corridor to the doorway on the left that leads into the briefing room.

Here's a tough fight: fire-breathing dogs accompany both Intermediate State MPs and MP Chiefs in search of your head on a platter. Transmute the two Tanks in the room and start blasting away.

Nab the **Fullmetal Bangle** in the center of the room in the middle of the circular desk. Head west to find a smaller side room with a **Relax-Herb**. Exit the briefing room back to the main hallway, turn left, and follow it around the floor. Make your way to a flight of stairs, but don't miss the **Lightning Element** near the bars just beyond the stairs (see map for its exact location). Grab it and head up the stairs.

STAGE 6:
NEW HIESSGART
CASTLE

Holding Cells

Fortress Compound
(South)

Fortress Compound
(North)

Fortress 1F

Fortress 2F (West)

Fortress 2F (East)

Fortress 3F (East)

Fortress 3F (West)

Fortress 3F (East)

Fortress 4F (East)

Fortress 4F (West)

Fortress 4F (East)

Fortress Rooftop

Sky Chimera

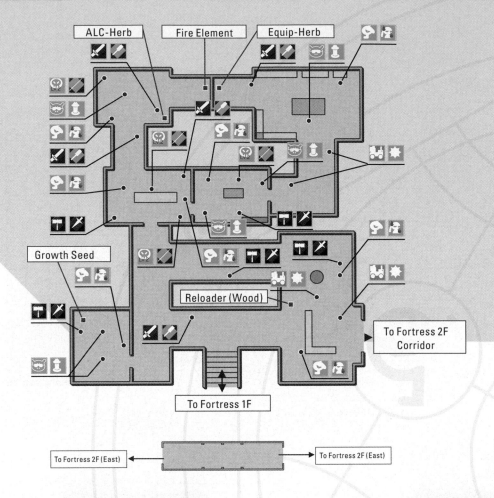

ALC-Herb   Fire Element   Equip-Herb

Growth Seed

Reloader (Wood)

To Fortress 2F
Corridor

To Fortress 1F

To Fortress 2F (East)   To Fortress 2F (East)

You can skip most of this floor if you're in a hurry, but if so, you'll miss out on some nice bonus items stashed in the back rooms. At the top of the stairs, turn right and head east to the

doorway that leads to the next area. Or you can go left (west) and explore; at the next intersection veer left and go into the small lounge in the southwest corner of the map. The room is empty, but when you enter, some MPs attack from behind. Wipe them out, then locate the **Growth Seed** in the lounge. Exit the lounge and turn left.

Go north into the training room filled with desks. Several MP Chiefs and their dogs attack. These close quarters offer a good opportunity for a Special Attack. Terminate the foes and continue to the room in the northwest corner to find a chest that holds an **ALC-Herb.**

Continue east into the corridor to find it blocked by steel bars. Grab the **Fire Element** from the chest near the bars, then retrace your steps back south to the training room with

all the desks. From there, go east through a big office with bookshelves into another hallway. Follow that around the corner into a large room with a big table in the center. Veer northwest to find **Equip-Herb** down the hallway with the steel bars. (You should be on the other side of the bars now.)

Now go back south to the stairway where you entered this floor. From there, go east into the lobby with the big round pillar. A squad of MPs guards this room, so defeat them and nab the

Reloader (Wood) item. Then exit via the eastern door. You enter the Fortress 2F Corridor, then a passage that leads to the eastern half of floor 2F.

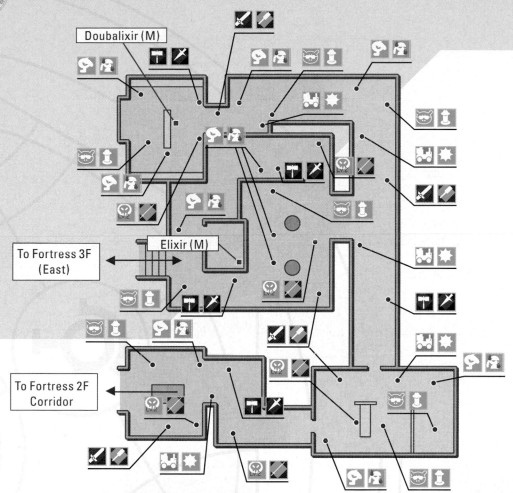

Doubalixir (M)

To Fortress 3F (East)

Elixir (M)

To Fortress 2F Corridor

GAME BASICS

COMBAT TACTICS

CHARACTERS

EQUIPMENT

ENEMIES

WALKTHROUGH

STAGE 1: CENTRAL RAILROAD

STAGE 2: REMINESS GORGE

STAGE 3: HIESSGART

STAGE 4: NEW HIESSGART, PART 1

STAGE 5: NEW HIESSGART, PART 2

STAGE 6: NEW HIESSGART CASTLE

STAGE 7: HIESSGART ARMY FORTRESS

STAGE 8: UNDERGROUND WATERWAY

APPENDIX

Fight through the first room, then transmute the Tank on the far side and drive it down the corridor to the next doorway. Fire shells into the next room, picking off all thrcc MPs before entering.

Go due north up the long corridor, stopping to transmute another Tank from an ash can. Ride the Tank north until you reach a ramp (about halfway down the hall) that leads down to a room on the left. Six MPs (three Chiefs, three Intermediate) suddenly pour out into the hallway! Back the Tank southward, firing north at the attackers while backpedaling.

After the MP assault is crushed, continue north to the end of the corridor and transmute yet another Tank. Hop onto it (or let Al drive) and spin around the corner, gunning down more MPs

and their dogs. Keep following the hallway until you reach a room with a **Doubalixir (M)** in front of some planters. Now go back down the long hallway to the ramp (now to the right) and descend it into a room with the two large circular pillars. Take the hallway that wraps around to the other side and get the **Elixir (M)** stashed in the small room opposite the stairs. Then climb the stairs up to the third floor.

FLOOR ROUTE

Security bars block direct access to parts of the fortress's third and fourth floors, but don't get frustrated. You can reach those parts, albeit in a roundabout way. The path (laid out in this walkthrough) takes you back and forth via connecting corridors from east to west on each floor.

STAGE 6:
NEW HIESSGART
CASTLE

Holding Cells

Fortress Compound
(South)

Fortress Compound
(North)

Fortress 1F

Fortress 2F (West)

Fortress 2F (East)

Fortress 3F (East)

Fortress 3F (West)

Fortress 3F (East)

Fortress 4F (East)

Fortress 4F (West)

Fortress 4F (East)

Fortress Rooftop

Sky Chimera

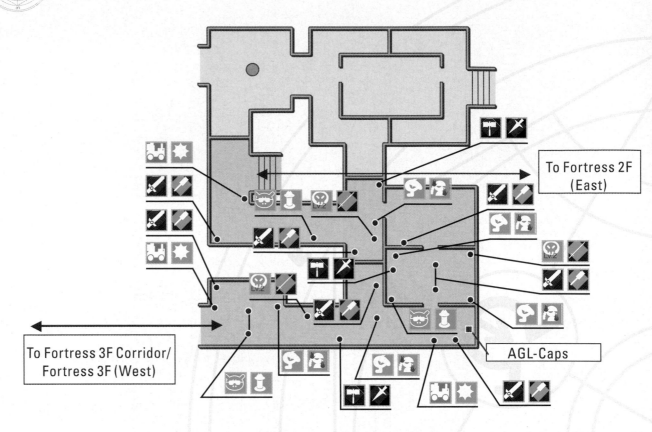

To Fortress 2F
(East)

To Fortress 3F Corridor/
Fortress 3F (West)

AGL-Caps

The path here is linear, so don't look for side rooms to explore. Walk left down the hallway, transmute a Tank, and drive it until you reach the dogs and blast them. Continue until you reach the large rooms with the glass walls. Those dark, gray-suited fellows on the other side of the glass are Senior State MPs with alchemy powers. Each one can transmute a yellow-green Gatling Gun for a short, painful burst.

Defeat the MPs in the room and go into the hallway to the south. Get the **AGL-Caps** on the eastern end and turn to face the Senior State MPs with swords. These alchemists can transmute an attack that sends a fiery fin zipping along the floor, causing damage when it comes in contact with anyone.

When they're history, follow the hallway down to the lobby, where a few MP Chiefs await with bated breath. Exit into the Fortress 3F Corridor after defeating these foes and proceed west to the next area.

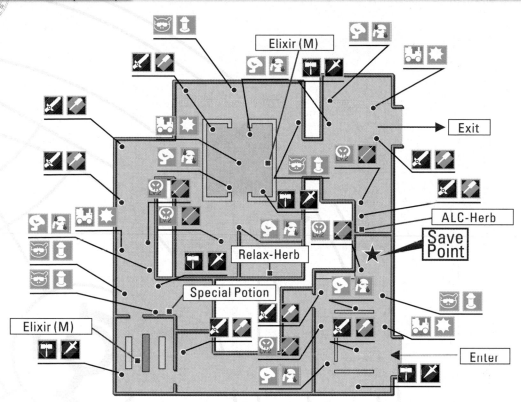

Elixir (M)

Exit

ALC-Herb

Save Point

Relax-Herb

Special Potion

Elixir (M)

Enter

GAME BASICS

COMBAT TACTICS

CHARACTERS

EQUIPMENT

ENEMIES

WALKTHROUGH

STAGE 1:
CENTRAL
RAILROAD

STAGE 2:
REMINESS GORGE

STAGE 3:
HIESSGART

STAGE 4:
NEW HIESSGART,
PART 1

STAGE 5:
NEW HIESSGART,
PART 2

STAGE 6:
NEW HIESSGART
CASTLE

STAGE 7:
HIESSGART ARMY
FORTRESS

STAGE 8:
UNDERGROUND
WATERWAY

APPENDIX

Hustle north and use the save point before you fight! Then fight off the horde of enemies, save again, and go into the next room through the door to the west. Follow the hallway until you reach another locker room and find the **Elixir (M).** Exit to the north.

In the next hallway, fight off the pack of dogs and MPs (a Special Attack works well here), then get the **Special Potion** in the alcove to the east. Continue north along the hallway until you reach a large open room patrolled by numerous enemies. Transmute Tanks for an extra punch. Get the **Elixir (M)** on the floor in the center area and a **Relax-Herb** in one of the storage areas to the south.

Proceed east into another heavily guarded lobby and, after crushing the resistance, get the **ALC-Herb** in the hall to the south. Exit via the east door to the next Fortress 3F corridor. Walk the length of the corridor and go through the door into the next area.

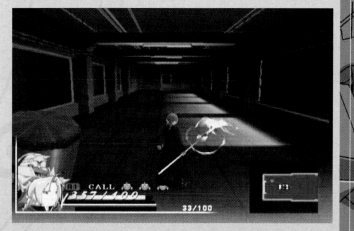

STAGE 6:
NEW HIESSGART
CASTLE

Holding Cells

Fortress Compound
(South)

Fortress Compound
(North)

Fortress 1F

Fortress 2F (West)

Fortress 2F (East)

Fortress 3F (East)

Fortress 3F (West)

Fortress 3F (East)

Fortress 4F (East)

Fortress 4F (West)

Fortress 4F (East)

Fortress Rooftop

Sky Chimera

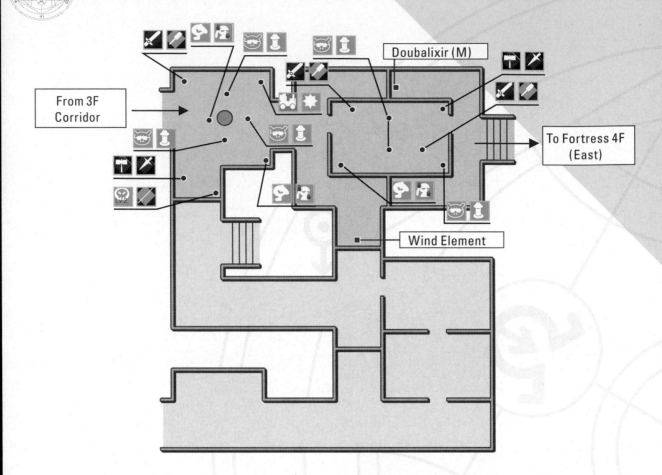

From 3F Corridor

Doubalixir (M)

To Fortress 4F (East)

Wind Element

This brings you back to the east side of the third floor, but now you should be on the other (northern) side of the security bars. Walk past the large circular pillar to the doorway of a room across the far hallway. The hallway wraps around this room but dead ends on both sides into locked gates. Turn right and follow the hallway around the southern bend to find a chest near the bars; it contains a **Wind Element**.

This room contains a couple of MP Chiefs with guns and grenades, a tough intermediate-level dog with its alchemic buzzsaw attack, and a deadly Senior State MP with his slashing sword. Exit the far door to face one last Senior State MP, this one with a gun (and his transmuted Gatling Gun attack). After you defeat him, go north along the hallway to a **Doubalixir (M)**, then return to the stairs and head up to the fourth floor.

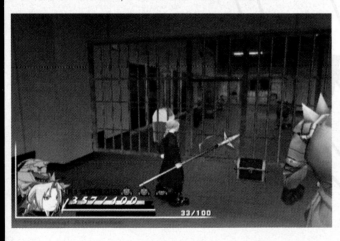

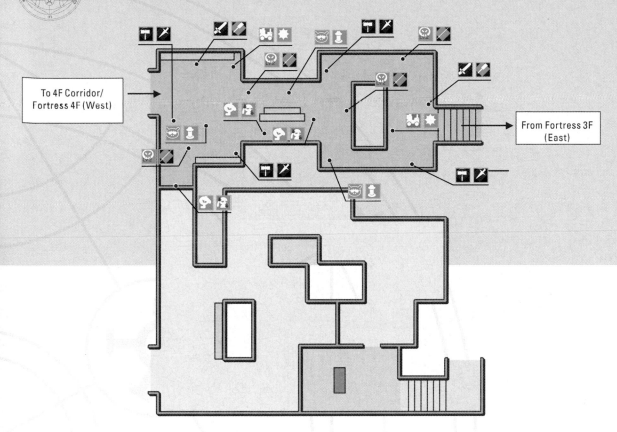

To 4F Corridor/Fortress 4F (West)

From Fortress 3F (East)

GAME BASICS

COMBAT TACTICS

CHARACTERS

EQUIPMENT

ENEMIES

WALKTHROUGH

STAGE 1:
CENTRAL
RAILROAD

STAGE 2:
REMINESS GORGE

STAGE 3:
HIESSGART

STAGE 4:
NEW HIESSGART,
PART 1

STAGE 5:
NEW HEISSGART,
PART 2

STAGE 6:
NEW HIESSGART
CASTLE

STAGE 7:
HIESSGART ARMY
FORTRESS

STAGE 8:
UNDERGROUND
WATERWAY

APPENDIX

Dogs patrol the halls up here. Fight them off and proceed west into the next room. Here you meet a new enemy, the Tank. A good tactic is to eliminate all other enemies in the area and save the Tank for last. It is slow and can take a lot of hits, so you can string together some awesome combos and earn a lot of bonus experience points. There are no treasure chests in this area, so when the last enemy falls, just exit west to the 4F corridor.

TANKS FOR THE EXP

With a Plastic Hammer and the right combination of accessories, you can gain lots of experience from hitting the enemy Tank. Equip Ed with the Ultra Combo Guide accessory to increase your EXP gained from normal and combo attacks and add the Training Manual to boost EXP gained by another 5 percent. Finally, equip Al with the White Loincloth to prevent him from attacking the Tank. (You want the vehicle to suffer a long, slow death!)

Now hammer away at the Tank with combo attacks of 50 hits per string, earning lots of bonus EXP. Just remember to stay away from the Tank's gun turret.

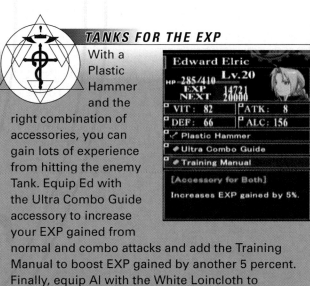

Edward Elric   Lv.20
HP 285/410
EXP 14721
NEXT 20000
VIT: 82   ATK: 8
DEF: 66   ALC: 156
Plastic Hammer
Ultra Combo Guide
Training Manual
[Accessory for Both]
Increases EXP gained by 5%.

**STAGE 6:
NEW HIESSGART
CASTLE**

Holding Cells

Fortress Compound
(South)

Fortress Compound
(North)

Fortress 1F

Fortress 2F (West)

Fortress 2F (East)

Fortress 3F (East)

Fortress 3F (West)

Fortress 3F (East)

Fortress 4F (East)

Fortress 4F (West)

Fortress 4F (East)

Fortress Rooftop

Sky Chimera

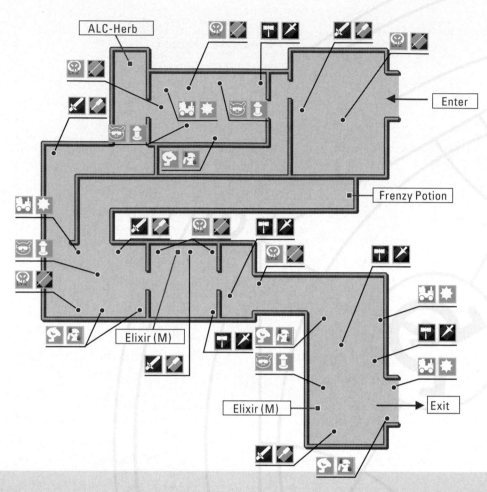

ALC-Herb

Enter

Frenzy Potion

Elixir (M)

Elixir (M)

Exit

Cross the room to the west doorway and step into the hallway. Around the corner, two dogs patrol a dead end. Wipe them out and enter the room. Another Tank is posted here. As before, eliminate the other enemies first using good weapons, then transmute the trash can into another Plastic Hammer and hit the Tank for hundreds (if not thousands) of EXP!

When the Tank finally explodes, go into the next hallway and open the chest in the north end for an **ALC-Herb**. Follow the hallway down to the next big room and defeat the squad of tough MPs. From that big room, find another doorway to the north (*not* the one you entered from) and follow the long hallway to a dead end with a **Frenzy Potion**. Then return to the big room and go east. The next room contains an **Elixir (M).**

Continue east to the lobby. Defeat the enemies (MPs, a dog, and a Tank) in your manner of preference and get the **Elixir (M)** next to one of the benches. Then exit via the east door into another 4F Corridor. Follow that east to the next area.

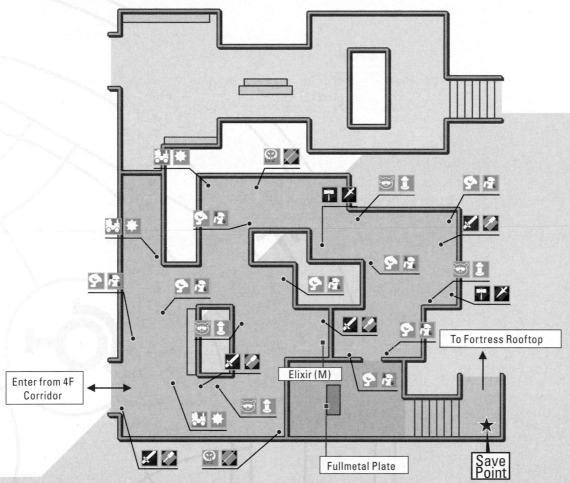

Enter from 4F Corridor

Elixir (M)

To Fortress Rooftop

Fullmetal Plate

Save Point

GAME BASICS

COMBAT TACTICS

CHARACTERS

EQUIPMENT

ENEMIES

WALKTHROUGH

STAGE 1: CENTRAL RAILROAD

STAGE 2: REMINESS GORGE

STAGE 3: HIESSGART

STAGE 4: NEW HIESSGART, PART 1

STAGE 5: NEW HIESSGART, PART 2

STAGE 6: NEW HIESSGART CASTLE

STAGE 7: HIESSGART ARMY FORTRESS

STAGE 8: UNDERGROUND WATERWAY

APPENDIX

Two Tanks and a handful of MPs and Two-Headed Dogs lie in ambush as you step into the first room. If you follow the hallway to the east, you'll pass a chest containing an **Elixir (M)**. Then head north to a corridor with yet another enemy Tank and continue until you reach a room with two flags over the doorway.

Enter the room to trigger a cut-scene—Al finds Ed's watch—but search the room afterwards for a **Fullmetal Plate** underneath the desk. Head up the stairs and save your game before you exit to the rooftop.

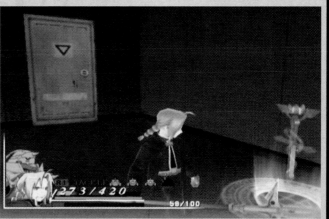

STAGE 6:
NEW HIESSGART
CASTLE

Holding Cells

Fortress Compound
(South)

Fortress Compound
(North)

Fortress 1F

Fortress 2F (West)

Fortress 2F (East)

Fortress 3F (East)

Fortress 3F (West)

Fortress 3F (East)

Fortress 4F (East)

Fortress 4F (West)

Fortress 4F (East)

Fortress Rooftop

Sky Chimera

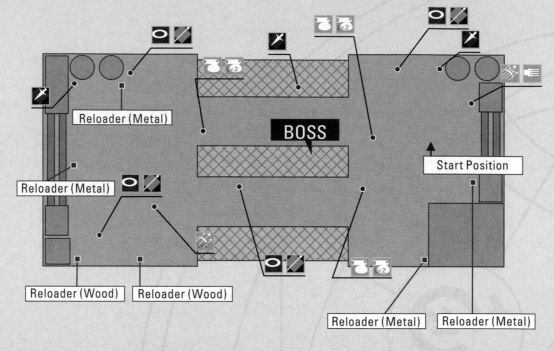

Reloader (Metal)

BOSS

Start Position

Reloader (Metal)

Reloader (Wood)   Reloader (Wood)

Reloader (Metal)   Reloader (Metal)

When you emerge onto the roof, a flying Sky Chimera swoops overhead. Ed and Al prepare for battle...

Sky Chimera

| HP | 1250 | HIT | 83 | SHOOT | 65 | ALC ATT | 55 | DEF | 45 |
| ALC DEF | 130 | EXP | 1500 | ITEM OBTAINED | Armlet of Strength | | | | |

GAME BASICS

COMBAT TACTICS

CHARACTERS

EQUIPMENT

ENEMIES

WALKTHROUGH

STAGE 1:
CENTRAL
RAILROAD

STAGE 2:
REMINESS GORGE

STAGE 3:
HIESSGART

STAGE 4:
NEW HIESSGART,
PART 1

STAGE 5:
NEW HIESSGART,
PART 2

STAGE 6:
NEW HIESSGART
CASTLE

STAGE 7:
HIESSGART ARMY
FORTRESS

STAGE 8:
UNDERGROUND
WATERWAY

APPENDIX

The Sky Chimera is blazing fast and only exposes itself to your attacks briefly, so fighting this boss keeps you on your toes. Access the Items menu and give AGL-Caps to both Ed and Al, then hustle to transmute Cannons (Level 2) from the gun-turrets on the roof. Have Al man one of the Cannons, but don't put Ed on one just yet.

Watch for the Sky Chimera to create a glowing transmutation circle on its chest. This indicates that it's about to spray fireballs. Avoid them by pressing the R2 button to dodge, and lure the bird closer to the ground so Al can get a clean Cannon shot.

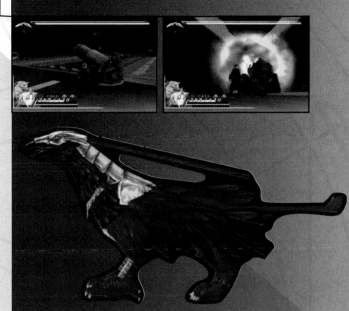

Don't forget to open the six Reloader chests (two Wood and four Metal) scattered around the rooftop.

When Al connects, the chimera will likely be stunned and drop briefly to the roof of the fortress. The key word here is *briefly*. Immediately mount another Cannon and *quickly* empty all four shots into the beast. Cannons deplete the

most HP from this boss (unless you're at a really high level), but note the other large weapons available to transmute on the rooftop. The Crossbow with its tracking arrows can also stun the Sky Chimera if you connect enough times. And if Ed's Alchemy stat is high, the Gatling Gun will also make short work of this boss.

Watch out for the bird's rocket-strafe attack as well as its overhead pass that unloads fireballs down on a large area of the map. Reload the Cannons while you're avoiding its other attacks and keep hitting this creature with those Cannons!

After the boss fight, Brigadier Nemda becomes livid at the loss of yet another of his beloved combat chimeras. He tries to stop the Elric boys from escaping, but Ed's alchemy is too clever.

Ed and Al return to the graveyard outside the church, where both Armony and the pastor greet their return.

STAGE 7:
HIESSGART ARMY
FORTRESS

Waterway A
Waterway B
Waterway C
Waterway D
Aqueduct
Sea Chimera

STAGE 7

UNDERGROUND

Back at the church, Armony explains that her father has kicked her out of the house. She thinks it's for practicing alchemy, but Wilhelm has other reasons for wanting her to leave the castle. The boys plan to rescue the professor from the military, but the town gates are blocked, so the pastor recommends using the sewer system walkways, which link the castle and the church.

Underground Waterway

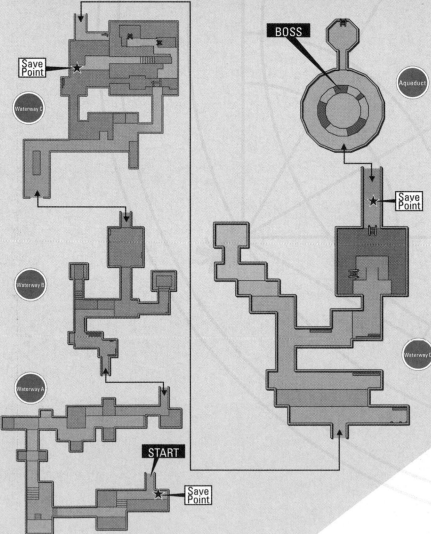

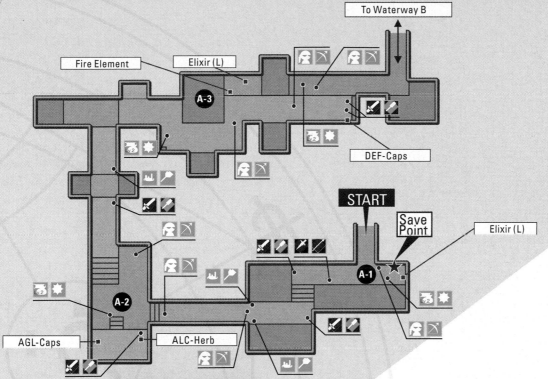

To Waterway B

Fire Element   Elixir (L)

DEF-Caps

A-3

START

Save Point

Elixir (L)

A-1

AGL-Caps   ALC-Herb

A-2

GAME BASICS

COMBAT TACTICS

CHARACTERS

EQUIPMENT

ENEMIES

WALKTHROUGH

STAGE 1:
CENTRAL RAILROAD

STAGE 2:
REMINESS GORGE

STAGE 3:
HIESSGART

STAGE 4:
NEW HIESSGART, PART 1

STAGE 5:
NEW HIESSGART, PART 2

STAGE 6:
NEW HIESSGART CASTLE

STAGE 7:
HIESSGART ARMY FORTRESS

STAGE 8:
UNDERGROUND WATERWAY

APPENDIX

The path through the waterways is linear, so don't worry about getting lost. You start in area A-1. Soon after you arrive, a wild pack of Two-Headed Dogs attacks. Wipe them out (transmuting the nearby Crossbow helps), then use the nearby save point. Open the treasure chest for an **Elixir (L)** and proceed down the tunnels to the water-filled corridor.

Transmute the barrier at the near end of the corridor into a Crossbow and let Al man it. Move down the corridor to lure various bandits (called Underground Bandits) into Al's range. Then move to the end of the corridor and repeat this tactic with the next barrier/Crossbow.

Upon reaching the room marked A-2 (look for a small crooked sign next to the large runoff), head up the steps to the south to find the **AGL-Caps** and **ALC-Herb** in a pair of treasure chests on the platform.

Proceed north up the ramp out of the water. More bandits patrol a water trench up ahead, including a few with rifles. Give Al some Grenades and fight to the other side of the trench.

When you reach the A-3 area where a huge circular pipe dumps water into the ground, fend off the dog and bandit ambush. Continue east around the bend and nail the enemy alchemists in the distance by transmuting a scrap pile into a Cannon (Lv. 2) and blasting them.

EVASIVE ALCHEMISTS

When facing the hooded alchemists, watch out for transmuted cages dropping from above. The cage drops on the glowing alchemy circles on the ground, so avoid it when you see one of them.

Now search for the **Elixir (L)** in the runoff to the north and a **Fire Element** in the water near it. Continue east across the bridge and find a **DEF-Caps** near the steel drums at the end of the walkway. Hop into the water and follow the waterway around the corner to the exit. Uh-oh! Looks like someone's following the boys...

STAGE 7: HIESSGART ARMY FORTRESS

Waterway A
Waterway B
Waterway C
Waterway D
Aqueduct
Sea Chimera

[Map of Waterway B]

To Waterway C

ATK-Caps

Fullmetal Ring

Elixir (L)

Equip-Herb

A-7

Relax-Herb

A-5

A-6

A-4

Doubalixir (L)

To Waterway A

Fight to the east until you reach the water level where the large runoff is located. Get ready for a wild swarm attack by numerous enemies. A good tactic is to transmute the two crates near the runoff into Quintuple Crossbows and immediately let Al man one, then run out and transmute the Suction Machine and quickly activate it. As Al decimates the enemies, let Ed man the other Crossbow and help him out.

From here, there are three corridors you can go down: A-5, A-6, and A-7. Let's just visit them in order.

A-5

At the water level, head west to the end of the waterway, then around the corner to the north and climb the stairs. This leads to a large sunken chamber. Jump down to nab the **Fullmetal Ring**. Back on the floating deck, the water begins to rise, bringing Ed back to the corridor level. Stay sharp, though! As the platform slowly rises, Killer Fish start hopping out of the water to attack.

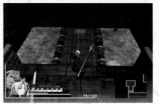

A-6

Return to the waterway and head due east into the A-6 corridor. Looks like a trap, doesn't it? Too good to be true? Relax, it isn't. Just walk out onto the platform and open the chests for a **Relax-Herb**, an **Elixir (L)**, and an **Equip-Herb**.

After the cut-scene in which Greta riles up the alchemist Outlaws in New Hiessgart, you start in the corridor marked A-4, where a group of Mercenaries in purple suits wield deadly blades or guns. Watch out for their alchemy attacks—they transmute a giant yellow fan that can suck you into its razor-sharp blades! Clean out the first area and look for a **Doubalixir (L)** in the southeast corner behind the pipes.

Continue deeper into the waterway until you reach the platform with a railing along its ledge. More Mercenaries and some nasty Electro-Slugs that spit electric bolts try to block your progress.

Finally, head down the A-7 central corridor into a stunning drainage area. Fighting here can be tricky because the falling water obscures enemy locations, so use a Special Attack if one is available. The Suction Machine in the center of the pool also comes in handy; use the nearby 5-shot Crossbow to punish foes clustered in a group.

Find the pipe in the center of the eastern wall that contains a chest with an **ATK-Caps;** note, however, that you'll need to create a Rockblocker to get into the pipe. Head north to exit the area.

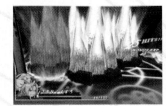
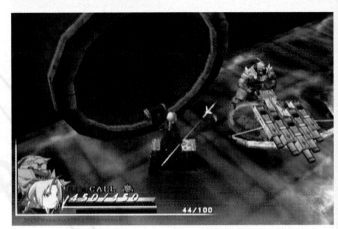

GAME BASICS

COMBAT TACTICS

CHARACTERS

EQUIPMENT

ENEMIES

WALKTHROUGH

STAGE 1: CENTRAL RAILROAD

STAGE 2: REMINESS GORGE

STAGE 3: HIESSGART

STAGE 4: NEW HIESSGART, PART 1

STAGE 5: NEW HIESSGART, PART 2

STAGE 6: NEW HIESSGART CASTLE

STAGE 7: HIESSGART ARMY FORTRESS

STAGE 8: UNDERGROUND WATERWAY

APPENDIX

WATERWAY C

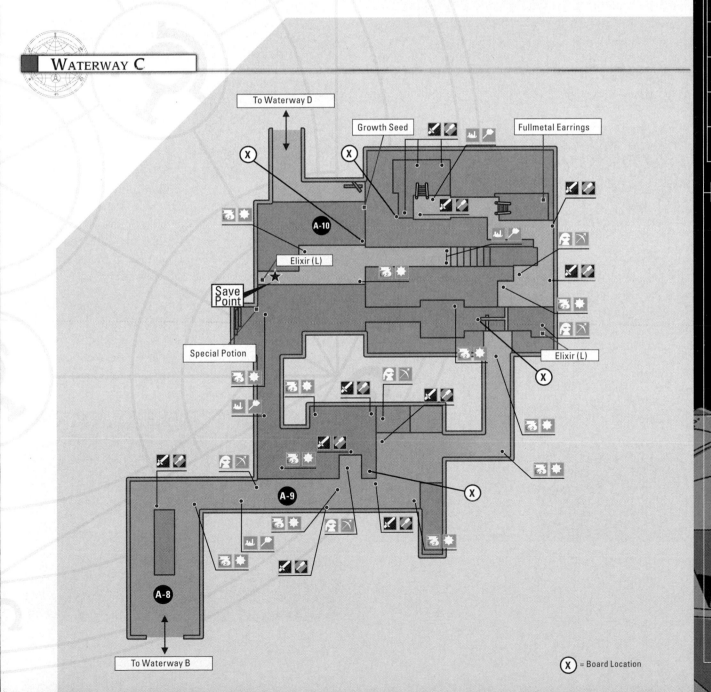

Waterway A
Waterway B
Waterway C
Waterway D
Aqueduct
Sea Chimera

Follow the steamy corridor north and east, fighting off aggressive Shellfish Chimeras capable of transmuting flying mech-bugs that explode in your face. At the corridor's end, there is an arched tunnel that slopes upward to the east. Skip that for now and hop down the "water steps" to the north. Be prepared for a very tough fight against more Shellfish plus a giant Military Crab.

FOUR BOARDS

To access Waterway D, you must find four boards in Waterway C. These are marked on the in-game map by a flashing yellow dot.

Why jump in the water first? You need a particular object here (guarded, unfortunately, by the Military Crab) before you can move on to Waterway D. It's a "hard board," marked on the in-game map by a yellow dot—the first of four boards you must acquire in this level. Destroy all of the Shellfish first, then battle the crab and grab the lumber. While still on the water level, head west and proceed through the tunnels to the north.

The next chamber is full of more disgusting Shellfish, so tear them apart. Then open the chest next to the steel beams near the west wall for a **Special Potion**. Go north through the arch marked A-10 and turn the corner to find a "strong board" marked by a yellow pointing arrow—the second of four boards you must gather. Careful! Grabbing the board triggers a Military Crab attack from behind!

Go back through the A-10 arch and turn left, bearing east. Cross two bridges and defeat *all* of the pink, bee-like Flying Puffers that appear because it makes things much easier later.

The Puffers seem to spawn endlessly, but they eventually stop appearing. Hang in there! Get to the corner and transmute a Crossbow for Al to use to quickly thin out the Puffer population.

FIGHT PUFFERS ON THE MOVE

The Lv. 2 version of the Flying Puffer will attempt to drop a transmuted cage, so keep moving! If you stand still even for a second, chances are good that a cage will trap you for a few precious seconds.

Look for a treasure chest with an **Elixir (L)** near the stone column. The walkway continues north and then turns west to a staircase, but avoid that path for the moment. Instead, return to the A-10 arch and go left (south), follow the passage back to the water-filled room, and hop up the water steps to the top floor. Now proceed east up the sloping arched tunnel that you passed earlier. Follow the passage to the section with exposed beams and chain-link fences around it.

Very carefully walk the beams to the "wooden board" indicated by the yellow arrow. (If you fall, you'll end up down where you fought all of the Flying Puffers!) Note: If you don't eliminate *all* of the pink Flying Puffers before you attempt this, they make the walk to the wooden board an extremely difficult experience.

You obtain a wooden board!

Turn around *slowly* and creep back to the double steel beams, then turn left and continue north to the other side of the platform. Follow the fenced walkway to an opening on the right to spot a stone column with ladder rungs. Jump down to the little island to find a chest with **Fullmetal Earrings**. Another swarm of Flying Puffers descends to attack, so swing away at them.

Use the ladder rungs to climb back up to the platform. Continue west along the walkway. At the end by the torch, jump down to another island to find the final board, the "dingy board," in a corner behind a barrel. Nab it, fight off the Shellfish Chimera pair that suddenly appears, then climb back up.

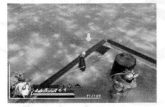 

Now return to where the exposed steel beams extend over the gap (where you found the wooden board) and jump down. Go east and follow the walkway around to the stairs but don't climb them yet. First, transmute the Crossbow on the platform and let Al man it. *Now* climb the stairs.

A big Military Crab guards the top of the stairs, and when you climb a few steps, another crab drops behind Ed, boxing him in! But this fight is easier than it looks. Al has Ed's back with the Crossbow; he nails the second crab. At the top of the stairs, two torches burn. Transmute one torch into a Sticky Oil canister and the other into a torch. Toss torches at the canister to break it and set the oil afire, annihilating the crab. Proceed west past the chain-link fence to an open platform where a yellow arrow points to a broken bridge.

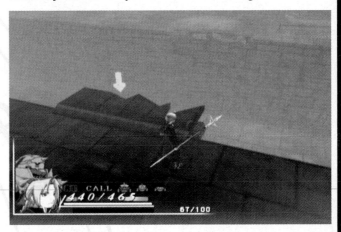

If you collected all four boards, you have enough wood to repair the bridge. Step to the yellow arrow and press the ◉ button to trigger the transmutation. After doing so, use the save point and get the **Elixir (L)** just to the west. Now cross the bridge into the next area where a **Growth Seed** rests inside a chest behind the fallen beams.

GAME BASICS

COMBAT TACTICS

CHARACTERS

EQUIPMENT

ENEMIES

WALKTHROUGH

STAGE 1:
CENTRAL
RAILROAD

STAGE 2:
REMINESS GORGE

STAGE 3:
HIESSGART

STAGE 4:
NEW HIESSGART,
PART 1

STAGE 5:
NEW HIESSGART,
PART 2

STAGE 6:
NEW HIESSGART
CASTLE

STAGE 7:
HIESSGART ARMY
FORTRESS

STAGE 8:
UNDERGROUND
WATERWAY

APPENDIX

STAGE 7:
HIESSGART ARMY
FORTRESS

Waterway A
Waterway B
Waterway C
Waterway D
Aqueduct
Sea Chimera

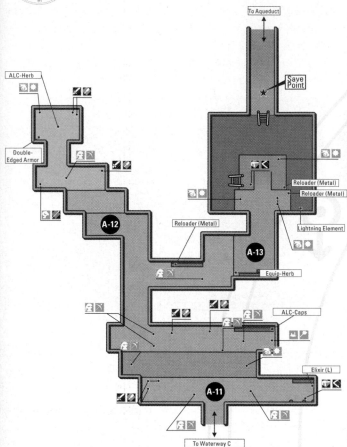

After the fight, find another chest with **ALC-Caps** atop another water pipe in the corner to the north of the trench. (Create a Rockblocker to get onto the pipe.) Now head west and turn north into the arched tunnel. Continue due north, ignoring the right turn (for now), until you reach the A-12 corridor.

Hop up the watery platforms, transmute the Crossbow, and walk past the two suits of armor into a chamber. From the entry, you can see a chest that contains an **ALC-Herb**. The moment you enter the chamber, however, three hostile Armored Knights turn blue and come to life. Soon after, two more knights who were standing guard at the chamber entrance join the fray. Defeat this small army, but notice that one knight doesn't come alive. See the chest behind him? You can't get it yet, but remember it for later.

Exit the A-12 corridor and take the first left, heading east to the A-13 corridor. On the way, look for the **Reloader (Metal)** item stashed beneath a large water pipe on the north wall. Just past the A-13 sign, locate an **Equip-Herb** tucked between the railing and the water pipe on the south wall of the room.

Welcome to section A-11 and meet the Female Knight, a purple-clad foe who features a swipe attack and an amusing alchemy attack—she transmutes a ball-and-chain that attaches to Ed's leg. This prevents Ed from fighting or running for a few seconds. Run east to transmute a barrier into a Crossbow for Al to use. Defeat the fiends and continue east to find a treasure chest with an **Elixir (L)** atop a pipe in the corner.

Go back to the west end and jump down into a real dogfight (literally) at the water level. Again, transmute a Crossbow at the west end of the canal for Al; there are more Crossbows

and a cannon if you proceed east along the trench, hopping up levels until you can jump out of the water to the north.

Turn the corner into a large water chamber and prepare for your first encounter with the boss, the Sea Chimera. This meeting is nothing compared to the next encounter with it, so breathe easy for now. Simply transmute the nearby debris piles into cannons and place both Ed and Al on their own cannon. Three or four shots should take care of the Sea Chimera this first time—the big beast shouldn't even get off an attack!

After the Sea Chimera runs off, turn around and get the **Reloader (Metal)** item just east of the ramp. Go up the ramp for another **Reloader (Metal)** (If you accidentally fall down into the water chamber, just go to the ladder on the west side of the platform and climb back up.) Now head back

into the tunnels and return to the A-12 chamber up in the northwest corner of the map.

Remember the chest that was previously inaccessible? The Armored Knight now attacks when you enter the chamber, thus providing access to the **Double-Edged Armor** he once blocked. After getting the item, return to the water chamber where you fought the boss. Drop down and look for the **Lightning Element** in the southeast corner. Go up the ladder to the north, save your game, and proceed to the next area.

TRANSMUTE A LANCE

Before you enter the Aqueduct, transmute a Lance and apply a Lightning Element to it. This saves time during the boss fight.

GAME BASICS

COMBAT TACTICS

CHARACTERS

EQUIPMENT

ENEMIES

WALKTHROUGH

STAGE 1: CENTRAL RAILROAD

STAGE 2: REMINESS GORGE

STAGE 3: HIESSGART

STAGE 4: NEW HIESSGART, PART 1

STAGE 5: NEW HIESSGART, PART 2

STAGE 6: NEW HIESSGART CASTLE

STAGE 7: HIESSGART ARMY FORTRESS

STAGE 8: UNDERGROUND WATERWAY

APPENDIX

AQUEDUCT

Exit

Double-Edged Bangle

Doubalixir (L)

BOSS

Reloader (Metal)

Doubalixir (L)

The moment you enter, the gate slams shut behind Ed and Al and the Sea Chimera emerges from one of this room's water pipes. Get ready for a wild, slithery battle!

BOSS FIGHT

STAGE 7:
HIESSGART ARMY
FORTRESS

Waterway A
Waterway B
Waterway C
Waterway D
Aqueduct
Sea Chimera

Sea Chimera

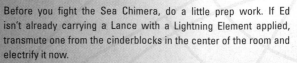

HP	3200	HIT	107	SHOOT	115	ALC ATT	93	DEF	58
ALC DEF	200	EXP	3000	ITEM OBTAINED	Armlet of Absorption				

Time for round two with the Sea Chimera, and this time four quick Cannon hits isn't going to cut it. But as with most bosses, the proper fighting techniques will send the Sea Chimera to an early watery grave.

This boss is slippery and darts from pipe to pipe, seeking an advantage. Be ready at any moment to press the R2 button to dodge. Its water-crystal attack (a volley of sharp icicles) is deadly and swift. Occasionally, the chimera sprays the room with a white vapor; sometimes it summons up geysers of water beneath your position on the grated platform. Lastly, the boss pops its snake-like head out of ceiling pipes to spew poisonous toxins. When this occurs, head to the opposite end of the room.

Before you fight the Sea Chimera, do a little prep work. If Ed isn't already carrying a Lance with a Lightning Element applied, transmute one from the cinderblocks in the center of the room and electrify it now.

Transmute a steel drum into a Steamroller and put Al at the wheel; he'll squash all the annoying Electro-Slugs that appear. This will enable you to focus most of your attention on the boss.

Next, transmute the three piles of debris in the chamber into Cannons and man the nearest one. Nailing the Sea Chimera with a cannonball should stun the creature for a few moments. When this happens, quickly hop off the Cannon, go behind the boss, and whack the beast with the Lightning Lance until it recovers and runs off. Repeat this process with the remaining Cannons and reload when necessary.

The three chests in the room contain two **Doubalixir (L)** items and a **Reloader (Metal).** After the boss fight, Ed and Al stay in this chamber, so you don't have to retrieve the items *during* the fight (unless you need them, of course).

Once the Sea Chimera falls in defeat, watch the cut-scene and go into the small chamber to the north. Nab the **Double-Edged Bangle** in the chest and climb the ladder to advance to the next stage.

STAGE 8

NEW HIESSGART CASTLE

Armony and the pastor join the Elric boys, and the foursome emerges from the sewers. They meet Professor Eiselstein in his castle and warn him of the warrant for his arrest by Brigadier Nemda. The professor explains the nature of his research on the Philosopher's Catalyst—the legendary substance that "improves transmutation efficiency and enables reconstruction that far exceeds the theoretical norm."

Then he reveals the secret of Armony's odd wing… and tells the heartbreaking story of what really happened to his daughter Selene. Ed and Al finally realize why Wilhelm has forbidden Armony from

practicing alchemy. Suddenly, the story is interrupted by commotion outside. Nemda and his "handler" are launching an all-out assault on the castle!

GAME BASICS

COMBAT TACTICS

CHARACTERS

EQUIPMENT

ENEMIES

WALKTHROUGH

STAGE 1:
CENTRAL RAILROAD

STAGE 2:
REMINESS GORGE

STAGE 3:
HIESSGART

STAGE 4:
NEW HIESSGART, PART 1

STAGE 5:
NEW HIESSGART, PART 2

STAGE 6:
NEW HIESSGART CASTLE

STAGE 7:
HIESSGART ARMY FORTRESS

STAGE 8:
UNDERGROUND WATERWAY

APPENDIX

CASTLE SQUARE

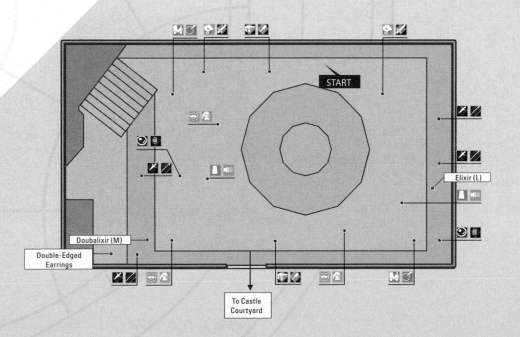

After the cut-scenes, Ed and Al end up in the Castle Square where military personnel begin to swarm. Three new foes appear: a burly Sentry armed with a sword, a Sentry with a handheld machinegun, and a slinking Hit Man with a razor Handblade.

Transmute various large weapons around the yard for Ed and Al, including a Poison Cow or two. Lure foes into their pink, bovine bubbles of death! You can also transmute your own Deadly Bubbles, if bubbles are your thing.

STAGE 8:
UNDERGROUND
WATERWAY

Castle Square
Castle Courtyard
Castle Square
Castle Foyer
Genz Bresslau
(Version 3)
Center Corridor
Area
Dining Hall Area
Great Hall Area
Tower Garden Area
Tower 2F Area
Tower 3F
Tower 3F Spiral
Stairs
Tower 3F Outer
Spiral
Tower 4F Area
Tower 4F
Spiral Stairs
Tower 5F Hub Area
Tower 5F Chamber 1
Castle Keep
Three Chimeras
Redux
Ultimate Chimera
and Camilla
Alchemyworks
Courtyard
Mustang and
Armstrong
Finale

After you defeat the enemies, get the **Elixir (L)** on the grass on the east side of the square, and the **Doubalixir (M)** on the southwest corner of the lawn. Head around to the steps to get the **Double-Edged Earrings** on the southwest corner on the porch, too. Exit through the gate in the south to trigger another cutscene.

CASTLE COURTYARD

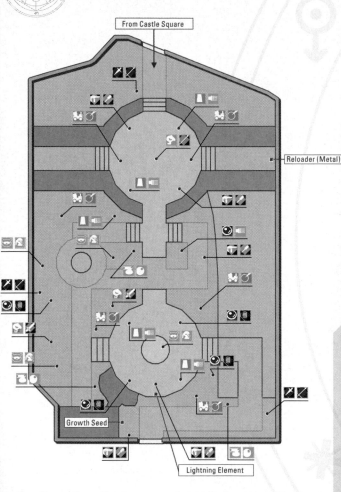

Now turn your attention to the foes. Enemy alchemists transmute spinning buzz-saws and razor-blade fans, or drop cages from above; big level-3 Bouncers unhinge their shotgun arms to blast Ed and Al; Hit Men sling their sneaky suitcase guns. Use alchemy liberally, as there are plenty of transmutable objects in the courtyard.

Gather items from the treasure chests first; you can't return to this map after you defeat all of the enemies. First, climb the steps to the circular platform and go to the left toward the east gate to get the **Reloader (Metal)** item. Now hustle to the other circular platform on the south end of the map and get the **Lightning Element** near the torch on the south side of the platform. Hop over the rail toward the gate to the south and turn west to find a chest underneath the windows with a **Growth Seed** inside.

When the last foe in the first enemy wave goes down, there is no breather as a second wave of opponents immediately pours into the courtyard. After defeating the second wave, a seemingly unbeatable third wave appears.

Things look bleak for the boys until Armstrong, Mustang, and Hawkeye come to the rescue.

GAME BASICS

COMBAT TACTICS

CHARACTERS

EQUIPMENT

ENEMIES

WALKTHROUGH

STAGE 1:
CENTRAL
RAILROAD

STAGE 2:
REMINESS GORGE

STAGE 3:
HIESSGART

STAGE 4:
NEW HIESSGART,
PART 1

STAGE 5:
NEW HIESSGART,
PART 2

STAGE 6:
NEW HIESSGART
CASTLE

STAGE 7:
HIESSGART ARMY
FORTRESS

STAGE 8:
UNDERGROUND
WATERWAY

APPENDIX

CASTLE SQUARE

Now back in the Castle Square the map is the same as before, except it has an added save point to the north, near the door into the castle. Defeat all of the enemies (the same assortment as the last time), then save your game. Or, try the tactic explained in the "Work Yourself into a Frenzy" tip. When you're ready, proceed north through the castle doors to fight Genz Bresslau for the last time.

WORK YOURSELF INTO A FRENZY

Here's a good way to prepare for the next boss fight: When fighting in the Castle Square, charge up Ed's

blue Frenzy Gauge until you activate a Fighting Frenzy, then carry that state of frenzy over into the boss fight in the next area, the Castle Foyer.

To do this, however, *you cannot save your game after the Castle Square fight.* Whenever you use a save point, you automatically lose any current Fighting Frenzy status. Instead, save your game early in the fight, and certainly no later than midway through the battle, while you still have plenty of enemies left to fight.

A good way to quickly fill up the Frenzy Gauge is to transmute a dagger and add a Wind Element to it. The speed of Wind Dagger strikes really builds great combo strings.

STAGE 8:
UNDERGROUND
WATERWAY

Castle Square

Castle

Courtyard

Castle Square

Castle Foyer

Genz Bresslau
(Version 3)

Center Corridor
Area

Dining Hall

Area

Great Hall Area

Tower Garden

Area

Tower 2F Area

Tower 3F

Tower 3F Spiral
Stairs

Tower 3F Outer
Spiral

Tower 4F Area

Tower 4F
Spiral Stairs

Tower 5F Hub

Area

Tower 5F

Chamber 1

Castle Keep

Three Chimeras
Redux

Ultimate

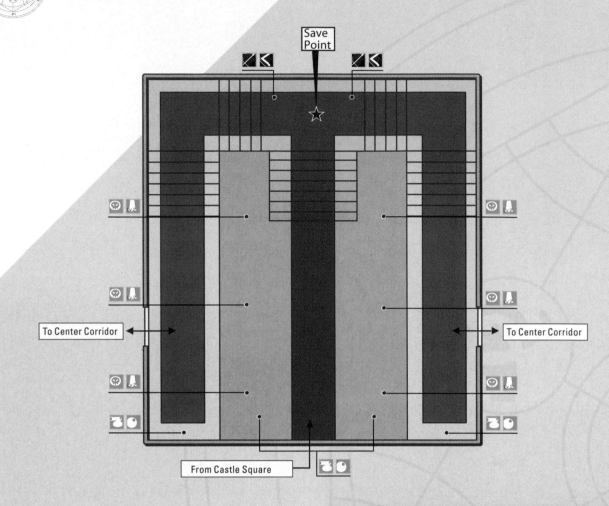

Save Point

To Center Corridor

To Center Corridor

From Castle Square

Genz looks somewhat frightening with his new full-automail overhaul. After the taunting dialogue exchange, the fight begins. Note: The save point that appears on the map becomes available only after the battle ends.

Genz Bresslau (Version 3)

HP	150	HIT	120	SHOOT	100	ALC ATT	78	DEF	999
ALC DEF	999	EXP	2000	ITEM OBTAINED	Flurry Guide				

If you have a Special Frenzy Attack available, *immediately* hold down the ● button to charge up Ed's Alchemy Gauge, run up the stairs toward Genz, and keep pressing the R1 button to keep Al close and eventually trigger the special. If it works, you can knock a huge chunk of HP off Genz's health gauge right off the bat.

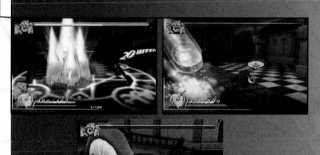

This last incarnation of Genz is the toughest one yet. All of his attacks are potent, and he bounds around the room in high, powerful leaps, making him difficult to track at times. Additionally, his DEF and ALC Defense stats are both maxed out, so fighting him is truly a lesson in patience. Most of your attacks inflict only 1 HP of damage per hit! But Genz saunters slowly between leaps, so take advantage of this to inflict damage.

Don't waste any Special Attacks on Genz unless they're Frenzy Special Attacks. The frenzy attack freezes Genz in place, so you get a guaranteed hit. But the standard Special Attack *doesn't* freeze Genz; he's free to move around and jump out of the way as the attack unfolds.

Genz's old attacks are deadly, but he's added some new ones to his arsenal, too. A nasty fireball attack, for example: Genz retreats to a corner or suspends himself in the air and summons balls of flame that descend from various angles. Genz now has a "mohawk" attack, too; he transmutes the mohawk atop his head into a huge blade and slashes at Ed and Al, sending shock waves along the floor too. Finally, when his HP gets low enough, Genz performs a devastating inferno attack; he stands in the middle of the room and flings volley after volley of fireballs in every direction.

GET BACK, JACK!

When Genz gets knocked to the ground, quickly hop away and keep your distance! As he slowly gets to his feet, he unleashes a brutal alchemy attack, thrusting sharp blades up from the ground all around him.

The key is to hit Genz from a distance. First, transmute all four statues into Cannons, two on the lower level and one on each side of the balcony. Use the floor Cannons liberally on Genz. The balcony Cannons can't hit Genz down on the floor, so use them only when Genz leaps up to the balcony. Dodge frequently to avoid his attacks as you move from Cannon to Cannon, and just reload when you run out of ammo.

Make sure Al has a weapon, as he will make some valiant attempts to combo-hit Genz. However, chances are good that Al will fall at least once in this battle if you don't heal him regularly.

If you run out of reloaders (a distinct possibility), transmute a Boomerang from the candleholders on the stairway, then transmute it again into a Razor Ring. Like the Boomerang, the Razor Ring can hit a target twice if you're accurate—once when you throw it through the target and once again when the ring returns to Ed. Unlike the Boomerang, however, you have *four* Razor Rings when you equip Ed with the weapon. So you can actually hit Genz multiple times per attack, keeping him on the defensive.

After Genz falls, Ed and Al remain in the Castle Foyer. The pastor appears and reports that Greta has taken Armony up to the castle keep—the highest tower in the castle. A save point appears at the north end of the room at the top of the stairs. Save your game and continue up to the west balcony. Exit via the door there.

Fortunately, although Genz has a high defense rating, he doesn't have much HP (only 150). You may not think you're making much progress by knocking only 1 HP off his health each time you hit him, but monitor his life meter during the battle. He'll drop sooner than you think.

GAME BASICS

COMBAT TACTICS

CHARACTERS

EQUIPMENT

ENEMIES

WALKTHROUGH

STAGE 1: CENTRAL RAILROAD

STAGE 2: REMINESS GORGE

STAGE 3: HIESSGART

STAGE 4: NEW HIESSGART, PART 1

STAGE 5: NEW HIESSGART, PART 2

STAGE 6: NEW HIESSGART CASTLE

STAGE 7: HIESSGART ARMY FORTRESS

STAGE 8: UNDERGROUND WATERWAY

APPENDIX

STAGE 8:
UNDERGROUND
WATERWAY

Castle Square
Castle Courtyard
Castle Square
Castle Foyer
Genz Bresslau
(Version 3)
Center Corridor
Area
Dining Hall Area
Great Hall Area
Tower Garden Area
Tower 2F Area
Tower 3F
Tower 3F Spiral
Stairs
Tower 3F Outer
Spiral
Tower 4F Area
Tower 4F
Spiral Stairs
Tower 5F Hub Area
Tower 5F Chamber 1
Castle Keep
Three Chimeras
Redux
Ultimate Chimera
and Camilla
Alchemyworks
Courtyard
Mustang and
Armstrong
Finale

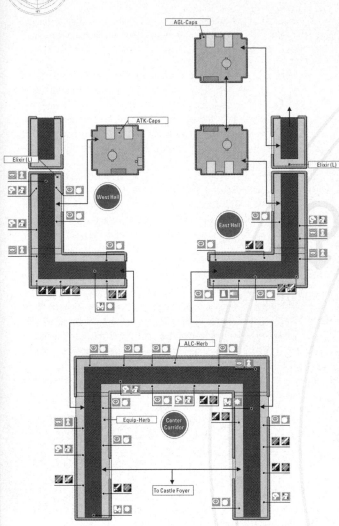

This portion of the walkthrough describes each section of the castle, along with its accompanying map. In this section, the Center Corridor is shaped like an upside down "U," with halls extending from its east and west sides. Several bedrooms lie just off the hallways.

Center Corridor

Bouncers, MPs, and Hit Men with suitcase guns congregate in the corridor. Transmute some weapons and wipe them out of the first length of hallway, then find the **Equip-Herb** across the hall from the northwest exit. Exit via the northwest exit.

West Hall 1

More minions lurk here, including some pink Female Knights (Level 2) plus a few hooded, cage-dropping alchemists. Fight around the corner to find the **Elixir (L)** at the end of the hall. Go through the next door.

Guest Bedroom

Look for the **ATK-Caps** between the beds and return to the Center Corridor. Be ready! All of the enemies along the route have re-spawned, thus forcing you to fight through all of them again.

Back to Center Corridor

Fight around to the eastern side of the Center Corridor but don't miss the **ALC-Herb** along the northern part of the hallway. Exit via the northeast door (the southeast exit takes you back to the Castle Foyer).

East Hall 1

More new enemies! Go up East Hall 1 through the sword-slashing Female Warriors as well as Sentries, Bouncers, and various alchemists. Then enter the door at the end.

Guest Chambers

Just passing through! Nothing in this room. Proceed through the door in the north instead.

Guest Bedroom

Score the **AGL-Caps** on the west side of the room, next to the bed. Exit to the east.

East Hall 1

In this small room, whack the Sentry, then open the chest near the south wall for an **Elixir (L)**. Exit to the north.

DINING HALL AREA

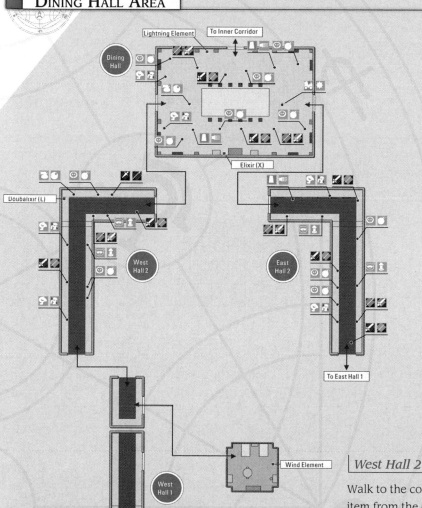

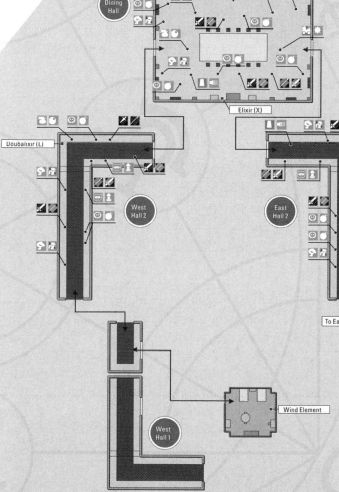

This area features a large dining room with hallways exiting east and west.

East Hall 2

Slash through the Sentries and Female Warriors and round the corner. Exit to the west.

Dining Hall

After defeating all of the enemies, look for the **Elixir (X)** on the south wall between the fireplace and a dining cabinet. Also, locate the **Lightning Element** to the left (west) of the northern exit, then take the western exit to explore the rest of the west wing of the castle.

West Hall 2

Walk to the corner of West Hall 2 and get the **Doubalixir (L)** item from the chest. Round the corner and exit to the south.

West Hall 1

This is an empty room! Simply exit to the east.

Guest Chambers

Open the chest in this room for a **Wind Element**. Exit the room to return to West Hall 1.

Back to the Dining Hall

Now retrace the route back to the Dining Hall, fighting through all of the respawned enemies. In the Dining Room, exit via the north door.

GAME BASICS

COMBAT TACTICS

CHARACTERS

EQUIPMENT

ENEMIES

WALKTHROUGH

STAGE 1:
CENTRAL
RAILROAD

STAGE 2:
REMINESS GORGE

STAGE 3:
HIESSGART

STAGE 4:
NEW HIESSGART,
PART 1

STAGE 5:
NEW HIESSGART,
PART 2

STAGE 6:
NEW HIESSGART
CASTLE

STAGE 7:
HIESSGART ARMY
FORTRESS

STAGE 8:
UNDERGROUND
WATERWAY

APPENDIX

STAGE 8:
UNDERGROUND
WATERWAY

Castle Square

Castle Courtyard

Castle Square

Castle Foyer

Genz Bresslau
(Version 3)

Center Corridor
Area

Dining Hall Area

Great Hall Area

Tower Garden Area

Tower 2F Area

Tower 3F

Tower 3F Spiral
Stairs

Tower 3F Outer
Spiral

Tower 4F Area

Tower 4F
Spiral Stairs

Tower 5F Hub Area

Tower 5F Chamber 1

Castle Keep

Three Chimeras
Redux

Ultimate Chimera
and Camilla

Alchemyworks
Courtyard

Mustang and
Armstrong

Finale

GREAT HALL AREA

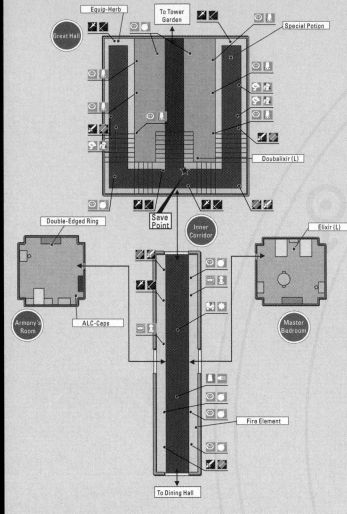

This next section runs down a long corridor to the Great Hall, with bedrooms on either side.

Inner Corridor

Quite an assortment of foes makes an appearance here, including two new types, Female Warriors Lv. 2 swing spiky balls on a chain, and Armored Knights Lv. 2 join the fray.

Don't miss the chest containing a **Fire Element** not far down the hall. Halfway along this corridor, two doors open on either side. The west door leads to Armony's Room, while the east door leads to the Master Bedroom. Enter them in any order.

Armony's Room

Look for a **Double-Edged Ring** inside the chest near the fireplace and an **ALC-Caps** item in the southeast corner of the room.

Master Bedroom

After you get the **Elixir (L)** in this bedroom, return to the Inner Corridor and exit to the north.

Great Hall

This hall is laid out the same as the Castle Foyer. Down below, there are two (Lv.3) Gator-Boars pacing on one side and two (Lv.2) Creeping Hodgepodges on the other side. Visit the eastern balcony to get a **Special Potion** and the western balcony for an **Equip-Herb**.

Now defeat the enemies below; female fighters (Warriors of both levels, plus Lv.2 Knights) join the battle as it rages. Be ready to dodge the Gator-Boar's brutal stone pillar alchemy attacks, and note that this level of Creeping Hodgepodge features the highest HP and alchemic ability in the castle. After clearing the room, grab the **Doubalixir (L)** on the main floor next to the staircase and use the save point at the top of the stairway. Exit to the north.

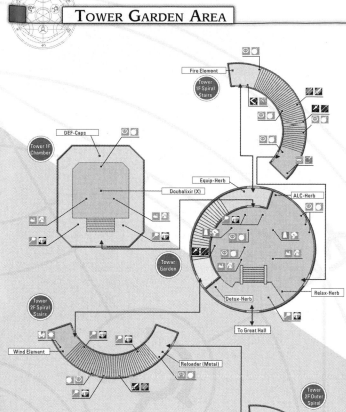

Find the **Detox-Herb** just to the left upon entering the area, and the **Relax-Herb** in the southeast corner near the wall. A third chest with an **ALC-Herb** is on the north side of the garden to the right of the door. Exit via the north door.

Tower 1F Chamber

Those pesky Winged Snakes drop from the ceiling of this room. Dodge their tornados and use a Special Attack to get rid of them quickly, then find the **Doubalixir (X)** and **DEF-Caps** before exiting the same way you came in. Once back in the Tower Garden, exit via the southeast door.

Tower 1F Spiral Stairs

Transmute the wood crate into a Steamroller and let Al man it to make defeating the chimeras on the stairs easier. Hustle upstairs and transmute the Crossbow, too. Look for a **Fire Element** at the top.

Tower Garden

You emerge onto the upper staircase level overlooking the Tower Garden, where a Female Warrior impedes your progress. Dispatch her and don't miss the **Equip-Herb** item next to the door as you come out. Take the stairs to the top and exit.

Tower 2F Spiral Stairs

Again, transmute a large weapon to make fighting the Gator-Boars easier; turn the sculpture into a Tank and fire away at the big chimeras. For the bothersome Winged Snakes, use a Special Attack if one is available. Get the **Wind Element** at the bottom of the steps, and don't miss the **Reloader (Metal)** item hidden behind the sacks at the top before you exit.

Tower 2F Outer Spiral

Quickly run through this area to avoid the crushing spike-blocks that drop from the ceiling and exit at the top.

GAME BASICS

COMBAT TACTICS

CHARACTERS

EQUIPMENT

ENEMIES

WALKTHROUGH

STAGE 1:
CENTRAL
RAILROAD

STAGE 2:
REMINESS GORGE

STAGE 3:
HIESSGART

STAGE 4:
NEW HIESSGART,
PART 1

STAGE 5:
NEW HIESSGART,
PART 2

STAGE 6:
NEW HIESSGART
CASTLE

STAGE 7:
HIESSGART ARMY
FORTRESS

STAGE 8:
UNDERGROUND
WATERWAY

APPENDIX

This section includes an interior garden at the bottom of the castle tower, plus an antechamber and two levels of the staircase that spiral up around the tower.

Tower Garden

Powerful Armored Knights (Lv.2) and Female Warriors (both levels) guard this large circular room, as do the hard-to-hit Winged Snakes (Lv.3) with their alchemic tornado attack. Here's a good place to transmute Sticky Oil canisters and break them, then transmute some Torches, lure foes into the oil (where they get stuck), and toss a Torch into their midst to burn them up. Another good trick is to transmute all of the Mines plus the nearby Suction Machine (adding a Fire or Wind Element). When you activate the suction, it not only pulls in enemies but the Mines, too!

STAGE 8:
UNDERGROUND
WATERWAY

Castle Square
Castle Courtyard
Castle Square
Castle Foyer
Genz Bresslau
(Version 3)
Center Corridor
Area
Dining Hall Area
Great Hall Area
Tower Garden Area
Tower 2F Area
Tower 3F
Tower 3F Spiral
Stairs
Tower 3F Outer
Spiral
Tower 4F Area
Tower 4F
Spiral Stairs
Tower 5F Hub Area
Tower 5F Chamber 1
Castle Keep
Three Chimeras
Redux
Ultimate Chimera
and Camilla
Alchemyworks
Courtyard
Mustang and
Armstrong
Finale

From this point, it's a one-way trip through rooms until you reach the next spiral stairway—that is, once you enter a room, the door locks behind you, so you can't backtrack. Connecting hallways give you a choice of rooms. In most cases, only one of the rooms contains items; this walkthrough describes the path to those rooms.

Tower 2F

In this first fork, transmute a Katana for Al, then take the door on the left (west).

Tower 2F Inner Chamber

One Armored Knight (Lv.3) stands guard in this room as you enter. Defeat him and do some prep work *before* opening the chest in the middle of the room. First, transmute and break the four Sticky Oil canisters, then get a Torch from the north end of the room. Now open the chest to obtain a **Doubalixir (X)**.

This triggers the release of more Armored Knights into the room! These foes are capable of one-hit kills, so keep your distance! Fortunately, they land right in the pools of Sticky Oil so toss some torches to burn them up! Exit to the north.

Tower 2F

Get the **Doubalixir (L)** near the middle of the south wall, and select the door to the east this time.

Tower 2F Inner Chamber

A **Doubalixir (X)** sits in the middle of this room, but two Armored Knights guard it. Before opening the chest, transmute the Crossbow from the statue and let Al man it. Transmute other objects (including some Dummy Eds) for easy use, then open the chest and jump into one of the Steamrollers to destroy the headless knights. Continue to the north.

Tower 2F

A chest rests on top of a pedestal on the south end of this room. Open it to obtain an **Elixir (X),** and exit through the lone doorway the north.

Tower 2F Spiral Stairs

Winged Snakes love stairwells, apparently, and here they bring a handful of bigger friends—Gator-Boars and the Creeping Hodgepodge menace. The Steamroller is perhaps the best option in these cramped quarters, so transmute one and create some chimera pancakes. You can also transmute Tanks from sculptures on the stairs for Ed. Nab the **Elixir (L)** at the bottom of the stairs, then continue to the top.

TOWER 3F

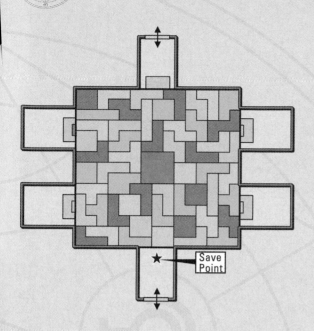

★ Save Point

Puzzle time! The floor blocks consist of four colors (red, blue, yellow, and green) that are configured in different shapes. The big square block in the center displays one of these four colors. When the cylindrical press drops onto the center block, then every floor block matching that center color falls away. If Ed is standing on one of the blocks that falls, he drops to the Tower 2F Outer Spiral room, forcing you to work your way back up.

AL'S COOL
Al disappears from the room during this process. Don't worry. He returns after you solve the puzzle.

To get past this room, you must trip all four of the color-marked switches in the room's side alcoves. Tripping a switch freezes the blocks of the corresponding color so they don't drop anymore.

The switch alcoves are too high to reach by jumping, not even if you use a Rockblocker. You can only reach a switch by jumping onto the rising block in front of it. Once you get into the alcove, walk up to the switch and press the ● button to activate it. After tripping all four switches, stairs appear in the north. Hop up the steps and exit the area.

GAME BASICS

COMBAT TACTICS

CHARACTERS

EQUIPMENT

ENEMIES

WALKTHROUGH

STAGE 1: CENTRAL RAILROAD

STAGE 2: REMINESS GORGE

STAGE 3: HIESSGART

STAGE 4: NEW HIESSGART, PART 1

STAGE 5: NEW HEISSGART, PART 2

STAGE 6: NEW HIESSGART CASTLE

STAGE 7: HIESSGART ARMY FORTRESS

STAGE 8: UNDERGROUND WATERWAY

APPENDIX

TOWER 3F SPIRAL STAIRS

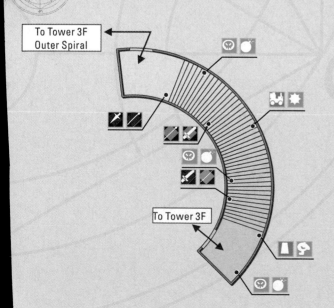

To Tower 3F Outer Spiral

To Tower 3F

Powerful foes patrol this stairway. Fight past the Gorilla-Goat and the Armored Knights to reach the top. Transmute the Tank halfway up the stairs for extra firepower.

STAGE 8:
UNDERGROUND
WATERWAY

Castle Square

Castle
Courtyard

Castle Square

Castle Foyer

Genz Bresslau
(Version 3)

Center Corridor
Area

Dining Hall
Area

Great Hall Area

Tower Garden
Area

Tower 2F Area

Tower 3F

Tower 3F Spiral
Stairs

Tower 3F Outer
Spiral

Tower 4F Area

Tower 4F
Spiral Stairs

Tower 5F Hub
Area

Tower 5F

Chamber 1

Castle Keep

Three Chime-
ras Redux

Ultimate

TOWER 3F OUTER SPIRAL

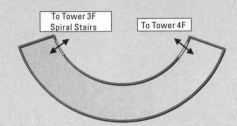

Spiked iron balls fall from a chute at the top of this curving ramp and roll down toward Ed. Hug the inner wall to avoid harm and reach the top unscathed. If a ball does happen to bounce your way, *dodge!*

TOWER 4F AREA

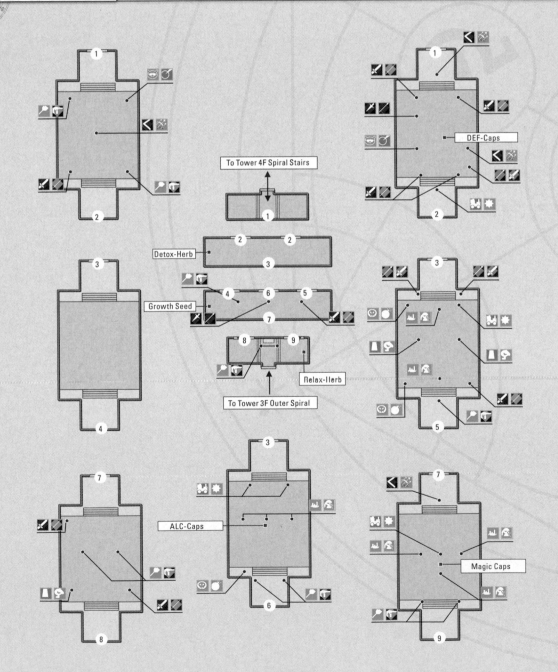

Time for some more one-way travel. As in the Tower 3F area, the doors lock behind you as you go from room to room. Again, this walkthrough guides the player along the path that holds the most goodies.

Tower 4F

Get the **Relax-Herb** on the east end of this room, and pick the door on the east (refer to door 9 on the map).

Tower 4F Inner Chamber

Use a quick Special Attack to thin out the Winged Snake infestation inside this room, then transmute a Crossbow for Al from the statue at the north end of the room. You can also transmute some Sticky Oil canisters and break them to slow down these speedy snake-like birds. Open the chest in the middle of the room for a **Magic-Caps**, then exit to the north.

Tower 4F

This time, you have three doors from which to choose. Pick up the **Growth Seed** on the west end of the room and go through the door in the center (door 6 on our map).

Tower 4F Inner Chamber

More hungry Gator-Boars await your entrance in this chamber. Transmute the pair of Tanks across the room and pair up with Al on the vehicles. Get the **ALC-Caps** in the middle of the room when you're through.

Tower 4F

Get the **Detox-Herb** on the west end of this room and select the door on the east (the rightmost door #2 on our map).

Tower 4F Inner Chamber

Transmute a Tank from the sculpture straight ahead as you enter, and unload lots of rounds into the four, big Gorilla-Goats. Get the **DEF-Caps** from the chest and exit to the north. In the next room, continue through the only door to the north.

GAME BASICS

COMBAT TACTICS

CHARACTERS

EQUIPMENT

ENEMIES

WALKTHROUGH

STAGE 1:
CENTRAL RAILROAD

STAGE 2:
REMINESS GORGE

STAGE 3:
HIESSGART

STAGE 4:
NEW HIESSGART, PART 1

STAGE 5:
NEW HIESSGART, PART 2

STAGE 6:
NEW HIESSGART CASTLE

STAGE 7:
HIESSGART ARMY FORTRESS

STAGE 8:
UNDERGROUND WATERWAY

APPENDIX

TOWER 4F SPIRAL STAIRS

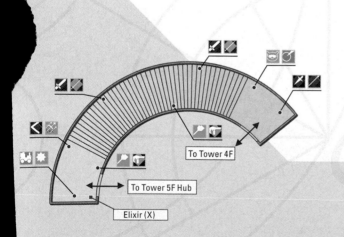

To Tower 4F

To Tower 5F Hub

Elixir (X)

Transmute the Steamroller at the bottom of the stairs and steamroll your way up to the top. There, you can make a Tank and a Crossbow and call Al to join Ed in some gruesome chimera destruction. Look for the **Elixir (X)** nearby before exiting.

133

STAGE 8: UNDERGROUND WATERWAY

Castle Square

Castle Courtyard

Castle Square

Castle Foyer

Genz Bresslau (Version 3)

Center Corridor Area

Dining Hall Area

Great Hall Area

Tower Garden Area

Tower 2F Area

Tower 3F

Tower 3F Spiral Stairs

Tower 3F Outer Spiral

Tower 4F Area

Tower 4F Spiral Stairs

Tower 5F Hub Area

Tower 5F Chamber 1

Castle Keep

Three Chimeras Redux

Ultimate Chimera and Camilla

Alchemyworks Courtyard

Mustang and Armstrong

Finale

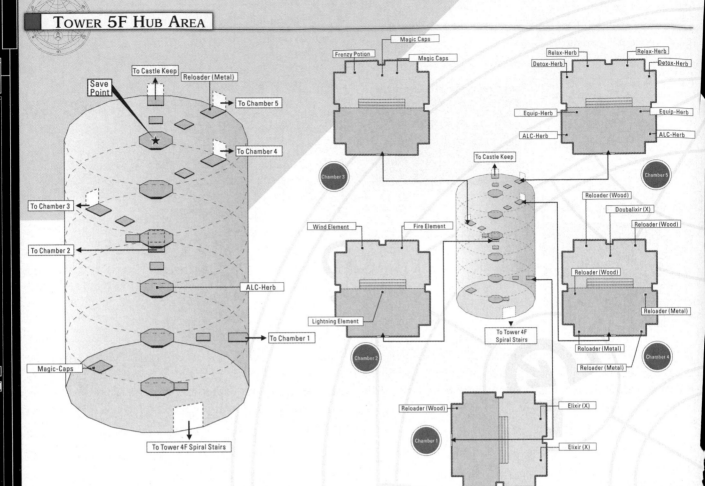

This next area provides a respite from fighting and lets you stock up for the final boss battles that lie ahead. The hub is a huge cylindrical chamber with six different levels that are accessible using orange, floating platforms. Platforms also ferry Ed and Al to a number of side chambers stocked with useful items.

Tower 5F Hub

Approach the small orange platform and hop onto it. As it automatically rises, turn to face the center of the room and step onto the first-level floating island.

Face east toward another orange platform that floats horizontally, moving back and forth between a far balcony and the center island. To reach the first chamber, jump onto this platform, but be careful; it doesn't move all the way to the center. Try to land on the platform as it comes toward you, ride it across, and go through the door on the other side.

Nab the three items inside this chamber: a **Reloader (Wood)** and two **Elixirs (X).** There are no foes to contest this easy plunder—no enemy soldiers, no chimeras, not a Winged Snake to be seen. Seems almost too easy, doesn't it? Exit back to the hub.

The Hub

Hop to the ground and let the orange platform on the ground level lift Ed and Al to the second-level center island, the one with a chest sitting on it. Hop over to open the **ALC-Herb** chest.

Note also the chest across the gap to the southwest, sitting on the balcony. You can't quite leap to it from here, but it is attainable from a better jumping point. For now, turn north and hop over to the moving orange platform and ride over to the second-level balcony to the north.

Tower 5F Chamber 2

Search the room for three elemental items: namely, a **Lightning Element**, a **Wind Element**, and a **Fire Element**. Head back to the hub.

The Hub

Jump down to the ground, get on the orange platform again, and ride it as high as it will go, stopping at the third center island of the hub. Step onto the island. On this level, there are two orange platforms, one to the west and another to the northwest.

The stationary platform (to the west) is a vertical lift, so hop northwest onto the moving platform to visit the next chamber.

Tower 5F Chamber 3

Three more items wait to be pillaged in this room: two **Magic-Caps** and a **Frenzy Potion**. Exit to the hub.

The Hub

Ride back across to the center island and step onto the other orange lift to make it rise. Ride up one level and step onto the next center island, the fourth level. The next chamber is to the northeast. Hop over to the moving platform and ride northeast to the far balcony. Go through the door.

Tower 5F Chamber 4

This treasure-filled chamber holds seven valuable items: three **Reloader (Metal)** items, three **Reloader (Wood)** items, and a **Doublalixir (X).** Return to the hub and ride over to the level 4 center island.

The Hub

This is a good place to go for the chest sitting on the balcony down on level 2. From the level 4 center island, face southwest and take a running leap of faith off the island. If you jump out far enough, you can just barely land on the level 2 balcony and nab the **Magic-Caps** from the chest.

Now jump to the ground, go ride the first vertical lift to its highest point, then walk onto the second vertical lift and ride it to its highest point at the fifth and final level. Yes, a save point!

On this level, the platform moving northeast/southwest shuttles its passengers to the last chamber in the hub. Before entering the chamber, open the chest on the ledge just outside the door for a **Reloader (Metal)** item.

Tower 5F Chamber 5

This last chamber is the most bountiful: two **ALC-Herbs**, two **Equip-Herbs**, two **Detox-Herbs**, and two **Relax-Herbs**. Exit to the hub and ride back to the top-level center island and save your game. Now ride the other orange platform across to the northern balcony.

GAME BASICS

COMBAT TACTICS

CHARACTERS

EQUIPMENT

ENEMIES

WALKTHROUGH

STAGE 1: CENTRAL RAILROAD

STAGE 2: REMINESS GORGE

STAGE 3: HIESSGART

STAGE 4: NEW HIESSGART, PART 1

STAGE 5: NEW HIESSGART, PART 2

STAGE 6: NEW HIESSGART CASTLE

STAGE 7: HIESSGART ARMY FORTRESS

STAGE 8: UNDERGROUND WATERWAY

APPENDIX

STAGE 8:
UNDERGROUND
WATERWAY

Castle Square

Castle Courtyard

Castle Square

Castle Foyer

Genz Bresslau
(Version 3)

Center Corridor
Area

Dining Hall Area

Great Hall Area

Tower Garden Area

Tower 2F Area

Tower 3F

Tower 3F Spiral
Stairs

Tower 3F Outer
Spiral

Tower 4F Area

Tower 4F
Spiral Stairs

Tower 5F Hub Area

Tower 5F Chamber 1

Castle Keep

Three Chimeras
Redux

Ultimate Chimera
and Camilla

Alchemyworks
Courtyard

Mustang and
Armstrong

Finale

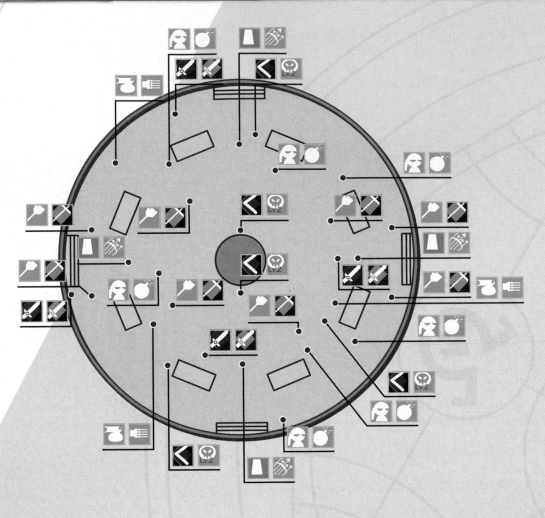

Here we go! Upcoming is a series of brutal boss battles against some familiar and unfamiliar foes. As the boys enter the castle keep's rooftop arena, Greta's betrayal and true identity become clear to all concerned. She turns loose some "old friends" and the first boss battle begins.

Three Chimeras Redux

Land Chimera		SHOOT	90	ALC ATT	90	DEF	70
HP	1700	HIT	95	ALC DEF	180	EXP	3000

Sky Chimera		SHOOT	110	ALC ATT	110	DEF	50
HP	1600	HIT	100	ALC DEF	185	EXP	3000

Sea Chimera		SHOOT	120	ALC ATT	110	DEF	55
HP	2000	HIT	110	ALC DEF	210	EXP	3000

ITEM OBTAINED Brawling Guide

Camilla's chimerical bosses of Land, Sea, and Sky now make a vengeful return. Individually, they bring nothing new—their attacks and patterns remain the same, plus each one's HP is lower. But now you face all three at once! Trying to transmute a bomb for the Land Chimera while avoiding a rain of fireballs from the Sky Chimera and, simultaneously, a stream of water crystals from the Water Chimera can be tricky. Likewise, causing damage to the other two bosses isn't easy when the Land Chimera is lobbing its tracker-fireballs.

Overall, the most important strategy here is *keep moving and dodging!* Fighting against three powerful attackers, Ed's health can drop quickly, so keep an eye on his HP and consume health items or herbs to cure status ailments.

Focus on a single boss until it drops, then turn your attention to another boss. The sooner you reduce the number of simultaneous attacks, the easier it becomes to manage your combat effectiveness.

Before the fight begins, use Magic-Caps on both Ed and Al to increase their stats—or, if you have no Magic-Caps, give AGL-Caps to Ed so he can escape the various attack volleys quicker. Transmute a basic Sword for Ed and add the Fire Element, as this will be the strongest weapon available. (Check the map for the four sword locations in the arena.) Transmute a weapon for Al as well.

Three crates in the arena can be transmuted into either a Cannon or a Gatling Gun. Choose the Cannon! Gatling Guns don't inflict much damage on these bosses. Exception: If you're trying to get a combo bonus, transmute one Gatling Gun. But this battle is *much* easier if you have at least two Cannons at your disposal.

You can defeat these three bosses in any order, but the Sea Chimera is perhaps the easiest to defeat first. Unlike the Flying Chimera, the Sea Chimera is a stationary target when it appears and, unlike the Land Chimera, its defense isn't particularly high. Here are some additional strategies for beating each boss:

Sea Chimera

Hop into the Cannon closest to where the Sea Chimera appears and start shooting. In the process, Ed may get knocked off the Cannon by attacks from the other two bosses. But as in the first fight with the Sea Chimera, once you hit this creature a few times, it remains stunned for a few seconds. Either rush up from behind and hack away with Ed's Fire Sword, or quickly reload the Cannon and unload again. Once the Sea Chimera falls, you remove its geysers and ice crystal attacks from the combat equation.

Sky Chimera

Next, try to attack the Sky Chimera. Again, this creature has a much lower defense than the Land Chimera, so it's more susceptible to damage and therefore falls faster. Reload the Cannons and wait for a clean shot. As in the first fight with the Sky Chimera, it falls from the sky stunned when you score a direct hit. Quickly reload and fire or rush the boss with Ed's Fire Sword. Watch for tracking fireballs from the other boss, and press the R2 button regularly to dodge while moving across the arena.

Land Chimera

Life is much easier when you don't have to dodge fireballs or water crystals, isn't it? Reload the Cannons (if you have any reloader items left) and blast the Land Chimera until it stops to eject its shells. When this occurs, sprint toward the shells nearest the beast's mouth, transmute one or two, and push them into the path of its vacuum attack. Basically, four swallowed bombs should do the trick.

Of course, while fighting these bosses, keep in mind that improvisation is sometimes the best approach. Don't pass up a golden opportunity to blast a boss just because it's out of your planned order. If you're near ejected shells as the Land Chimera is gearing up for its vacuum attack, transmute a bomb or two! If you're focusing on the Sea Chimera and the Sky Chimera suddenly looms in front of you, *nail it!*

GAME BASICS

COMBAT TACTICS

CHARACTERS

EQUIPMENT

ENEMIES

WALKTHROUGH

STAGE 1:
CENTRAL RAILROAD

STAGE 2:
REMINESS GORGE

STAGE 3:
HIESSGART

STAGE 4:
NEW HIESSGART, PART 1

STAGE 5:
NEW HIESSGART, PART 2

STAGE 6:
NEW HIESSGART CASTLE

STAGE 7:
HIESSGART ARMY FORTRESS

STAGE 8:
UNDERGROUND WATERWAY

APPENDIX

**STAGE 8:
UNDERGROUND
WATERWAY**

Castle Square

Castle Courtyard

Castle Square

Castle Foyer

Genz Bresslau
(Version 3)

Center Corridor
Area

Dining Hall Area

Great Hall Area

Tower Garden Area

Tower 2F Area

Tower 3F

Tower 3F Spiral
Stairs

Tower 3F Outer
Spiral

Tower 4F Area

Tower 4F
Spiral Stairs

Tower 5F Hub Area

Tower 5F Chamber 1

Castle Keep

Three Chimeras
Redux

Ultimate Chimera
and Camilla

Alchemyworks
Courtyard

Mustang and
Armstrong

Finale

Well, that battle is over—but as it turns out, this victory may be bittersweet. Camilla wanted her chimera's terminated, and she plans to use their sacrifice for her nefarious purposes. As Camilla tries to take what she desires from poor Armony, the professor makes a valiant effort to disrupt the plan.

Camilla's setback triggers her vicious, desperate response—the rise of the Ultimate Chimera. Are you playing right into Camilla's hands? Perhaps you'd better deal with her directly...

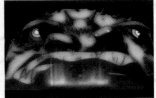

Ultimate Chimera and Camilla

Ultimate Chimera				SHOOT	140	ALC ATT	60	DEF	50
HP	1000	HIT	100	ALC DEF	180	EXP	1000		
Camilla				SHOOT	140	ALC ATT	120	DEF	70
HP	2500	HIT	120	ALC DEF	180	EXP	5000		

ITEM OBTAINED	Moon Medal

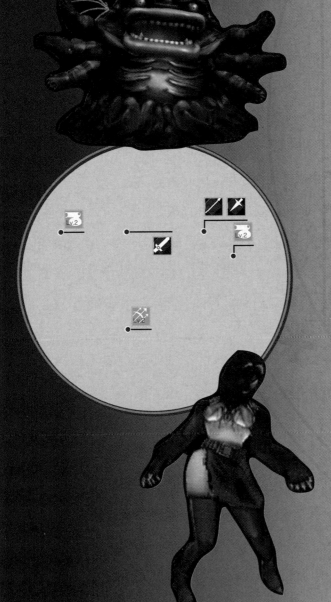

This final boss fight is a wild one. Camilla is fast and strong, and her Ultimate Chimera unleashes large area attacks and also inflicts status ailments. Despite the intimidating appearance of the monstrous creature, the task here is to defeat Camilla. When she goes down, the fight is over. Unfortunately, Camilla has n[o] visible HP bar, so it's tough to tell how close she is to death. The H[P] bar at the top of the screen is for the Ultimate Chimera.

The Ultimate Chimera is somewhat weak for a boss, but Camilla will revive her creation as many times as you defeat it. Plus, the big chimera's presence makes fighting Camilla a trickier task. However, there are two Cannons available in this fight, and a few well-placed cannonballs can quickly knock out the Ultimate Chimera. As soon as the creature falls, turn your full attention to Camilla.

It may not be in your best interests to let AI man a Cannon, since his Cannon attacks cause less damage than Ed's. In fact, if Ed's alchemy stat is high enough, four shots from the Cannon should knock out the Ultimate Chimera.

Again, Camilla is quick and powerful. She sprints around the arena and creates waves of energy that run along the ground, knocking Ed or Al. (They're easy to avoid by dodging.) Camilla also takes to the sky and unleashes a barrage of crystals. When she descends, she creates a vortex and throws herself on top of her targets, creating a shockwave with an area effect that can cause damage even if you manage to avoid the direct impact.

Start by using another dose of Magic-Caps or AGL-Caps on Ed. Transmute a Lance and put a Lightning Element on it. A Lightning Lance inflicts decent damage on Camilla, plus you can add Stonespikes to the combo attack. This creates a longer combo because Stonespikes juggle her in the air. (If you try the Stonespikes combo with the sword, you'll find that once you knock Camilla down, she disappears into the ground and reappears in another part of the arena.)

To defeat Camilla, chase her as she runs around the room, dodging when she creates her energy waves. Try to get in a few hits with the Lightning Lance when you get close. When she flies into the air, get as far away as possible to avoid her crystals. If Camilla creates a vortex, dodge and move in a straight line away from her. Once she's back on the ground, she'll take a few moments to recover; this is your chance to attack her. If Al is in the area, he can add to the combo.

After the Ultimate Chimera goes down, Camilla eventually creates a cloud of pink/purple particles, which indicates she's trying to revive her creation. As the chimera returns to life, it may emit an explosive yellow beam that can inflict poison status, so keep dodging and use the proper recovery items when necessary. Reload the nearest Cannon and knock out the creature again, then return your focus to Camilla.

You'll know Camilla's HP is getting low when she starts using new attacks. At this point, Camilla may create black balls of energy that circle the arena. Contact with them damages Ed or Al, so avoid them at all cost. Next, Camilla may create clones of herself, which attack from multiple sides. Just be mindful of Ed and Al's HP and continue to attack her.

GAME BASICS

COMBAT TACTICS

CHARACTERS

EQUIPMENT

ENEMIES

WALKTHROUGH

STAGE 1:
CENTRAL
RAILROAD

STAGE 2:
REMINESS GORGE

STAGE 3:
HIESSGART

STAGE 4:
NEW HIESSGART,
PART 1

STAGE 5:
NEW HIESSGART,
PART 2

STAGE 6:
NEW HIESSGART
CASTLE

STAGE 7:
HIESSGART ARMY
FORTRESS

STAGE 8:
UNDERGROUND
WATERWAY

APPENDIX

...r the fight, Professor Eiselstein asks Ed and Al to recover ...ving feathers scattered around the arena. Marked with ...ow arrows, they're easy to find. Just run through each ...ather to scoop it up. After collecting all 10 feathers, save ...your game.

FIND THE GRINDSTONE

As you circle the arena picking up feathers, pay attention to the ground. If the Ultimate Chimera is dead when Camilla dies, it *may* drop a rare accessory called the **Grindstone**. When equipped by Al, it gives him unlimited use of weapons (*except* the Katana).

There's only a random chance that the Ultimate Chimera will drop the Grindstone, so if you really want it, you *may* have to load a previous save and fight the boss fights again until it appears!

STAGE 8: UNDERGROUND WATERWAY

Castle Square

Castle Courtyard

Castle Square

Castle Foyer

Genz Bresslau (Version 3)

Center Corridor Area

Dining Hall Area

Great Hall Area

Tower Garden Area

Tower 2F Area

Tower 3F

Tower 3F Spiral Stairs

Tower 3F Outer Spiral

Tower 4F Area

Tower 4F Spiral Stairs

Tower 5F Hub Area

Tower 5F Chamber 1

Castle Keep

Three Chimeras Redux

Ultimate Chimera and Camilla

Alchemyworks Courtyard

Mustang and Armstrong

Finale

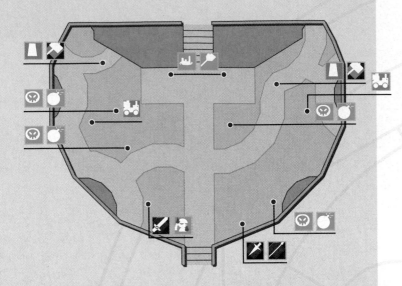

Ah, but the story's not finished yet! As the boys rush to "save" the professor and Armony, they're met at the Alchemyworks entrance by their military superiors, Colonel Mustang and Major Armstrong. The two officers refuse to allow passage into the lab. But Ed will not be denied, and is willing to disregard direct orders to get to Armony.

BOSS FIGHT

Mustang and Armstrong

Mustang		SHOOT	200	ALC ATT	170	DEF	175
HP	6999	HIT	130	ALC DEF	340	EXP	9999

Armstrong		SHOOT	150	ALC ATT	160	DEF	195
HP	9999	HIT	200	ALC DEF	380	EXP	9999

ITEM OBTAINED Moon Medal

Before reading any further, rest assured that you have already beaten the game. In this last fight against Mustang and Armstrong, you are not required to defeat them to see the end of the game. As a matter of fact, chances are very good that you *won't* beat *either one* this time around. Trying to fight these powerful bosses without being at a very, very high level is nearly impossible. Mustang and Armstrong are easily the toughest foes in the game, and just because they're the good guys doesn't mean they'll go easy on you.

To put it into perspective, Mustang has 6999 HP and Armstrong has 9999 HP. Unless you've nearly maxed out all of your stats, most of your attacks will inflict a measly 1 HP of damage per hit against either target. To make it worse, Mustang is nearly *impossible* to hit because he can evade almost any attack.

The Tank is perhaps the most semi-effective weapon in this fight. You can create two of them here. Transmute the lampposts on the east and west sides of the area.

Jump aboard and fire away, reloading when necessary if you have any reloaders left. (Chances are good you depleted them in the previous two boss fights.) Tank shells actually do *some* damage to the two master alchemists. But don't let them destroy the tank while you're in it!

The spoils of victory may be the only motivating factor for enduring the long, brutal war of attrition required to win this fight. Armstrong drops the **Demon Fist** when you defeat him, while Mustang drops the **Glass Samurai** when he falls. Note that you can only pick up one of the two items. If by some chance you defeat *both* Mustang and Armstrong in the same fight, the game jumps right to the "Boss Defeated" screen after the second foe falls and negates any chance to get the second item. Thus, you must play the game at least twice if you want to win every single item in the game.

If you really want to defeat one of them, target Armstrong. He may have a lot of HP, but at least you can hit him. Begin by consuming an AGL-Caps item, then create two Tanks, one on either end of the courtyard. If you've accrued any Bonus Points, put all of them into your ATK attribute. Hop into a Tank and unload everything into Armstrong before he gets close. When he does, *immediately* leave the Tank, because the vehicle takes damage only as long as you're manning it. Run over to the other side and mount the other Tank and repeat the process.

Continue this Tank-to-Tank tactic until you run out of Reloader (Metal) items. After this, you'll have to fight Armstrong hand to hand. The quickest weapon you can have is the Wind Dagger. Try to get around him to inflict damage.

Armstrong unleashes three main attacks. He can punch the ground to transmute three rock spikes. His energy geyser creates a blue wave across the ground. Finally, he uses his combo punches in close-quarters.

While you're engaging Armstrong, watch out for Colonel Mustang and his awesome fireball attack. When he says "Stand back!," you know he's preparing to shower the area. He can also create floating fireballs similar to Camilla's, except his attacks have greater volume and frequency. Finally, Mustang calls forth a deadly meteor shower that covers the entire field. To avoid it, you must rush to the farthest point on the map. Good luck!

GAME BASICS

COMBAT TACTICS

CHARACTERS

EQUIPMENT

ENEMIES

WALKTHROUGH

STAGE 1:
CENTRAL
RAILROAD

STAGE 2:
REMINESS GORGE

STAGE 3:
HIESSGART

STAGE 4:
NEW HIESSGART,
PART 1

STAGE 5:
NEW HIESSGART,
PART 2

STAGE 6:
NEW HIESSGART
CASTLE

STAGE 7:
HIESSGART ARMY
FORTRESS

STAGE 8:
UNDERGROUND
WATERWAY

APPENDIX

FINALE

Win or lose against Mustang and Armstrong, you get to watch the game's graceful ending sequences. Enjoy! And don't miss Lieutenant Hawkeye's comprehensive report after the game credits run... or the final scene on the Central train platform.

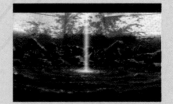

APPENDIX
UNLOCKING SPECIAL MOVIES AND GRAPHICS

The game manual mentions the Gallery feature that is available at the game's start menu. Here's how it works: After you complete the full game the first time and save that game at the end, you can play through a second time (loading the "Game Cleared" save game) to unlock special movies and graphics.

To unlock these movies and graphics, you simply open various treasure chests along the way during a second playthrough of the game. Then, when you save your game at the next Save Point, you automatically save any movies or graphics you've unlocked. Next time you return to the start menu (from "Game Over" after Ed is defeated or when you boot the PS2 to start a new game), you can select the Gallery option, open a saved game from your second playthrough, and choose either Movie or Graphic to view what you've unlocked so far.

You can unlock a total of 17 movies and 56 graphics during a second playthrough of the game. The maps in this appendix reveal the locations of every movie and graphic available in the game.

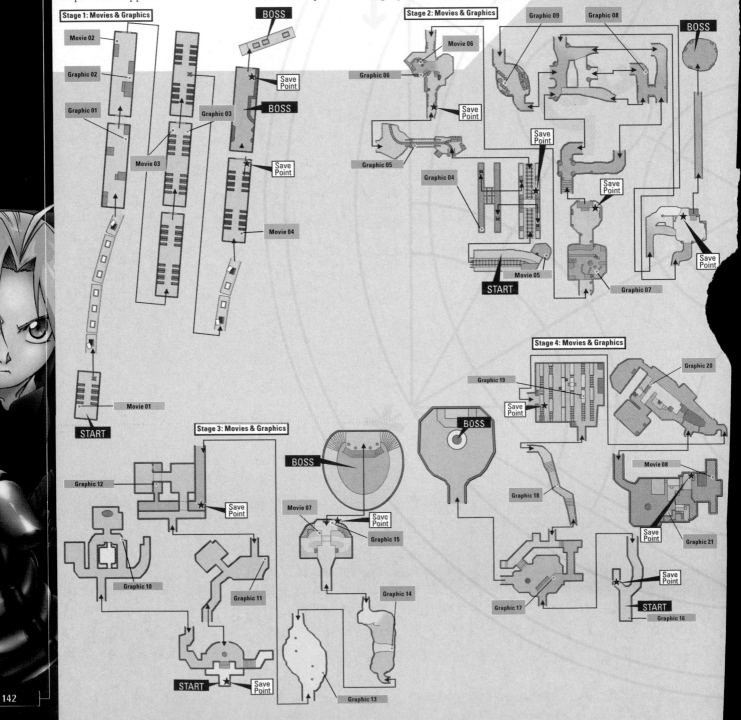

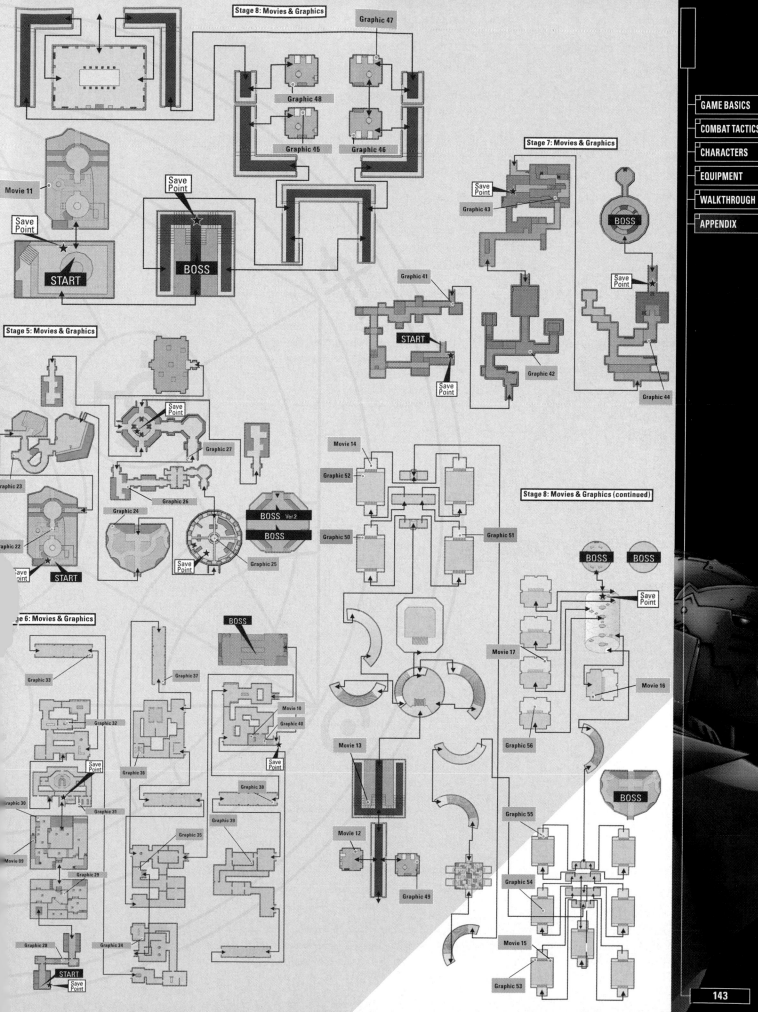

Stage 8: Movies & Graphics

Graphic 47

Graphic 48

Graphic 45   Graphic 46

Stage 7: Movies & Graphics

Movie 11

Save Point

Save Point

BOSS

START

Save Point

Graphic 43

BOSS

Graphic 41

Save Point

START

Save Point

Graphic 42

Graphic 44

Stage 5: Movies & Graphics

Save Point

Graphic 27

Graphic 23

Graphic 26

Graphic 24

BOSS Ver 2

BOSS

Graphic 22

Graphic 25

Save Point

Movie 14

Graphic 52

Stage 8: Movies & Graphics (continued)

Graphic 50

Graphic 51

Save Point

START

BOSS   BOSS

Save Point

Save Point

Movie 17

Movie 16

Stage 6: Movies & Graphics

BOSS

Graphic 33

Graphic 37

Graphic 32

Movie 10

Graphic 40

Graphic 36

Save Point

Save Point

Graphic 38

Graphic 56

Graphic 30

Graphic 31

Graphic 39

Graphic 55

Movie 13

Movie 09

Graphic 35

BOSS

Graphic 29

Graphic 54

Movie 12

Graphic 28   Graphic 34

Graphic 49

Movie 15

START

Save Point

Graphic 53

GAME BASICS

COMBAT TACTICS

CHARACTERS

EQUIPMENT

WALKTHROUGH

APPENDIX

BradyGAMES® Publishing

An Imprint of Pearson Education
800 E. 96th Street
3rd Floor
Indianapolis, Indiana 46240

ISBN: 0-7440-0496-9

Library of Congress Catalog No.: 2004114678

Printing Code: The rightmost double-digit number is the year of the book's printing; the rightmost single-digit number is the number of the book's printing. For example, 05-1 shows that the first printing of the book occurred in 2005.

08 07 06 05   4 3 2 1

Manufactured in the United States of America.

FULLMETAL ALCHEMIST
—and the Broken Angel—

OFFICIAL STRATEGY GUIDE

by Rick Barba

BradyGAMES Staff

Publisher
David Waybright

Editor-In-Chief
H. Leigh Davis

Marketing Manager
Janet Eshenour

Creative Director
Robin Lasek

Director of Marketing
Steve Escalante

Licensing Manager
Mike Degler

Assistant Marketing Manager
Susie Nieman

Team Coordinator
Stacey Beheler

Credits

Title Manager
Tim Cox

Development Editor
Chris Hausermann

Screenshot Editor
Michael Owen

Book Designer
Doug Wilkins

Production Designer
Wil Cruz

Author Acknowledgments

My thanks go to Leigh Davis for keeping me in the fold with yet another great project, and to my tag-team editors Tim Cox and Chris Hausermann, who continue to prove that BradyGames has the best editorial staff in this business, and that's by far. Thanks and love also to my family, who's support through thick and thin (and thinner) have made everything, every moment, worthwhile.